PARTY & BUFFET
COOKBOOK

PARTY & BUFFET
COOKBOOK

CELEBRATE IN STYLE WITH MORE THAN
90 RECIPES FOR SPECIAL GATHERINGS

CHRISTINE INGRAM

southwater

This edition is published by Southwater,
an imprint of Anness Publishing Ltd,
Hermes House, 88–89 Blackfriars Road,
London SE1 8HA; tel. 020 7401 2077;
fax 020 7633 9499

www.southwaterbooks.com;
www.annesspublishing.com

If you like the images in this book and
would like to investigate using them
for publishing, promotions or
advertising, please visit our website
www.practicalpictures.com for
more information.

Publisher: Joanna Lorenz
Managing Editor: Judith Simons
Art Manager: Clare Reynolds
Editor: Charlotte Berman
Recipes: Catherine Atkinson, Alex Barker, Oona van den Berg, Carla Capalbo, Jacqueline Clarke, Trish Davies, Joanna Farrow,
Christine France, Silvana Franco, Shirley Gill, Nicola Graimes, Rosamund Grant, Carole Handslip, Christine Ingram, Patricia Lousada,
Lesley Mackley, Sally Mansfield, Katherine Richmond, Laura Washburn, Steven Wheeler, Kate Whiteman and Elizabeth Wolf-Cohen
Photographers: Karl Adamson, Edward Allwright, Steve Baxter, Ian Garlick, Michelle Garrett, John Heseltine, Amanda Heywood, Dave Jordan,
Dave King, Don Last, William Lingwood, Patrick McLeavey, Michael Michaels, Thomas Odulate, Sam Stowell and Polly Wreford
Designers: Bill Mason, Jane Coney
Illustrator: Anna Koska
Editorial Reader: Richard McGinlay
Production Controller: Christine Ni

UK distributor: Book Trade Services; tel. 0116 2759086; fax 0116 2759090; uksales@booktradeservices.com;
exportsales@booktradeservices.com
North American distributor: National Book Network; tel. 301 459 3366; fax 301 429 5746; www.nbnbooks.com
Australian distributor: Pan Macmillan Australia; tel. 1300 135 113; fax 1300 135 103; customer.service@macmillan.com.au
New Zealand distributor: David Bateman Ltd; tel. (09) 415 7664; fax (09) 415 8892

ETHICAL TRADING POLICY
Because of our ongoing ecological investment programme, you, as our customer, can have the pleasure and reassurance of knowing that a tree
is being cultivated on your behalf to naturally replace the materials used to make the book you are holding. For further information about this
scheme, go to www.annesspublishing.com/trees

Previously published as *Celebrate in Style – Party Food*

NOTES
Bracketed terms are intended for American readers.
For all recipes, quantities are given in both metric and imperial measures and, where appropriate, in standard cups and spoons.
Follow one set of measures, but not a mixture, because they are not interchangeable.
Standard spoon and cup measures are level. 1 tsp = 5ml, 1 tbsp = 15ml, 1 cup = 250ml/8fl oz.
Australian standard tablespoons are 20ml. Australian readers should use 3 tsp in place of 1 tbsp for measuring small quantities.
American pints are 16fl oz/2 cups. American readers should use 20fl oz/2.5 cups in place of 1 pint when measuring liquids.
Electric oven temperatures in this book are for conventional ovens. When using a fan oven, the temperature will probably need to be
reduced by about 10–20°C/20–40°F. Since ovens vary, you should check with your manufacturer's instruction book for guidance.
Medium (US large) eggs are used unless otherwise stated.

Main front cover image shows Assorted Canapés – for recipe, see pages 54–5.

PUBLISHER'S NOTE
Although the advice and information in this book are believed to be accurate and true at the time of going to press, neither the authors
nor the publisher can accept any legal responsibility or liability for any errors or omissions that may have been made nor for any
inaccuracies nor for any loss, harm or injury that comes about from following instructions or advice in this book.

Contents

Introduction

Whether you are having a dinner party for a few close friends and family members, or celebrating a birthday or anniversary with 20 or 30 guests, party planning is essential for a successful celebration. Many parties celebrate a specific event, and in some cases, such as Thanksgiving, Diwali and Christmas, this means that you can follow a traditional structure for both the food and the decorations. Other parties are celebrations of birthdays or other anniversaries, and sometimes you might want to throw a party for no particular reason at all. On these occasions you probably need to put more thought into where and when to have the party, who to invite, what food and drink to serve and what decorations to choose – perhaps you want to have a themed event.

The following pages are packed with indispensable advice on party planning, plus ingenious and easy-to-make toppings and spreads, and suggestions for classic cocktails, including alcohol-free ones. This practical information, combined with 90 delicious recipes for snacks and nibbles, terrines, salads and desserts will ensure that your party is perfect in every way.

Types of parties

Any gathering of friends can be considered to be a party, but a coffee morning is obviously a very different event to a wedding celebration. If you are thinking of inviting just a few people you can have either an informal lunch or supper, or a more elaborate dinner party. Don't forget to let your guests know what type of party it is, as no-one likes to be over- or under-dressed. Most people don't have the space or furniture to accommodate more than eight or ten guests for a formal sit-down meal, so if you want to invite more than a handful of guests, buffet parties, barbecues or cocktail parties are probably best. Remember to keep an eye on the weather though, as barbecues in the rain are never a great success, and nor are indoor parties on a sweltering summer day.

Location and atmosphere

If you are having a stand-up party in your home, make the most of the space by putting furniture to one side or removing it completely. Ensure that anything that you are worried about getting broken is put away in a safe place. For a dinner party, it is easy to create an elegant atmosphere with some simple flower decorations and candles. Seasonal fruit, vegetables and flowers can create particularly striking and imaginative centrepieces. Finally, if you think your party will be noisy, check with your neighbours first.

Food and drink

Make sure that the food and drink you provide is suited to the occasion. Take into account the time of day, location, event, number of guests, expected length of the party and your budget. If guests are expected to stay only an hour or so, pre- or post-lunchtime, light snacks or canapés are perfectly adequate. For a buffet, you will need to prepare a variety of meat and vegetable dishes and desserts, but avoid serving too many hot dishes, as they will soon become cool. Whatever the event, make sure that you have a range of soft and alcoholic drinks, and don't let your guests' glasses stand empty.

Party pitfalls and how to avoid them

◆ Don't make dishes for a buffet party that appear complicated to serve, as they may make guests feel inhibited about attempting to help themselves. Food that doesn't need cutting with a knife is perfect for help-yourself parties.

◆ Avoid cumbersome canapés by keeping them bitesize. Finger food should be just that – food for eating with your fingers, but don't forget to provide plenty of napkins.

◆ Prevent salads from becoming soggy by serving the dressing separately.

◆ Avoid shortfalls by hiring plenty of glasses and buying wine on a sale or return basis from a local wine merchant.

◆ Don't let cold drinks become warm. Make large chunks of ice in margarine tubs or similar containers; they will melt more slowly than small cubes so will keep bowls of punch cooler for longer.

◆ Prevent damage to furniture by covering the serving table with a protective cloth, and reduce the chance of accidentally dropped glasses shattering by covering hard floor surfaces with rugs.

Classic Cocktails & Champagne Tips

Creating a classic alcoholic or non-alcoholic cocktail may take a bit more time than just opening a bottle of wine or pouring some orange juice, but your guests are certain to appreciate the effort.

Kew Pimms

A very drinkable concoction of sweet vermouth, curaçao, vodka, gin and cherry brandy served over assorted summer fruits.

To make 1 Kew Pimms put 1 measure/25ml/1½ tbsp sweet vermouth, 1 measure/25ml/1½ tbsp orange curaçao, ⅔ measure/15ml/1 tbsp vodka, ⅔ measure/15ml/1 tbsp gin and ⅔ measure/15ml/1 tbsp cherry brandy into a bar glass of ice and stir well. Strain into a tall highball glass full of ice and add some assorted summer fruits, mint leaves, 1–2 dashes of angostura bitters and equal amounts of American dry ginger ale and lemonade to taste.

To make the lemon triangle decoration cut a slit ¾ of the way across a rectangle of lemon rind. Turn the rectangle and repeat from the other side. Twist to form a triangle.

Frozen Strawberry Daiquiri

A version of the Cuban original, which was made with only local Cuban rum, lime juice and sugar. When out of season, used drained, canned straw-berries instead.

To make 4 Frozen Strawberry Daiquiris blend 225g/8oz/2 cups hulled strawberries with 5ml/1 tsp caster (superfine) sugar in a blender or food processor then press the purée through a sieve into a bowl. Return the purée to the blender with 5 measures/120ml/4fl oz/½ cup rum, 1⅓ measures/30ml/2 tbsp lime juice and 4 scoops of luxury strawberry ice cream. Blend until smooth. Put a scoop of luxury strawberry ice cream into 4 small glasses and pour over the blended mixture. Top up with lemonade and decorate with fresh strawberries and lime slices.

Vodka & Kumquat Lemonade

A mild-sounding name for a stong concoction of kumquat and peppercorn vodka and white curaçao.

To make 2 Vodka & Kumquat Lemonades thickly slice 75g/3oz kumquats and add to 5 measures/120ml/4fl oz/½ cup vodka in an airtight jar with 3 cracked black peppercorns. Set aside for at least 2 hours. Fill a jug (pitcher) with cracked ice and then add ⅔ measure/15ml/1 tbsp white curaçao or orange syrup, ⅔ measure/15ml/1 tbsp lemon juice and the kumquat and peppercorn vodka with the sliced kumquats and stir well. Add 7 measures/150ml/⅔ cup/¼ pint sparkling mineral or soda water and a few fresh mint leaves and stir everything together. Pour the drink into chilled glasses of ice and decorate with mint sprigs and slices of kumquats.

Steel Works

A thirst-quenching non-alcoholic drink, which is ideal to serve at any time of the day. The passion fruit adds an unusual flavour and texture to the drink.

To make 1 Steel Works pour 2 measures/ 45ml/3 tbsp passion-fruit cordial straight into a long glass. Add a dash of angostura bitters and two or three ice cubes to the glass before topping up the drink with 3 measures/ 70ml/4½ tbsp chilled soda water and 3 measures/70ml/4½ tbsp lemonade. Stir the drink gently. Cut a passion fruit in half, scoop the seeds and flesh from the fruit and stir into the drink. Stir the drink gently before serving.

Scarlet Lady

This cosmopolitan drink could easily pass as an alcoholic wine-based cocktail. For a longer drink, top up the fruit juice with extra grape juice and soda water.

To make 1 Scarlet Lady put 115g/4oz Honeydew, Galia or watermelon, 5 red grapes and 3 measures/70ml/4½ tbsp unsweetened red grape juice into a blender and process until smooth. Strain the juice into a bar glass of ice and stir until chilled, then pour into a chilled cocktail glass.

To make the decoration dip 3 red grapes into lightly beaten egg white then roll them in caster (superfine) sugar and secure them on a cocktail stick (toothpick).

St Clements

Freshly pulped orange and lemon create a very refreshing non-alcoholic cocktail. If preferred, you can use pineapple, peach or grape pulp instead.

To make 1 St Clements wash an orange and a lemon, thinly pare off their rind and remove and discard their pith. Put the rind in a pan with 15g/½oz sugar and 75ml/5 tbsp water. Heat gently until the sugar has dissolved then press the orange and lemon rind against the side of the pan to release all their oils. Remove the rind and leave the syrup to cool. Purée the orange and lemon and add the syrup. Sieve the fruit pulp and pour into a glass filled with crushed ice.

Opening and pouring champagne

Many people are still intimidated about opening sparkling wines. Remember that the longer a bottle of bubbly has been able to rest, the less lively it will be. If it has been badly shaken up, it may need a week or more to settle. Also, the colder it is, the less likely it will be to go off like a firecracker.

Once the foil has been removed and the wire cage untwisted and taken off, grasp the cork firmly and take hold of the lower half of the bottle. The advice generally given is to turn the bottle rather than the cork, but in practice most people probably do both (twisting in opposite directions, of course). Work very gently and, when you feel or see the cork beginning to rise, control it every millimetre of the way with your thumb over the top. It should then be possible to ease it out without it popping. If the wine does spurt, put a finger in the neck, but don't stopper it up again.

When pouring, fill each glass to just under half-full, and then go round again to top them up once the initial fizz has subsided. Pour fairly slowly so that the wine doesn't foam over the sides. Do not pour into tilted glasses: you aren't serving lager!

Spreads, Toppings & Breads

It is surprisingly simple to make delicious spreads and toppings from everyday food staples, such as soft cheese, garlic or tomatoes. Try serving them as fillings for mini croissants, spread on toasted ciabatta, or stuffed in pitta bread pockets to make popular party food.

Avocado Spread

This filling is particularly suitable for open sandwiches, croissants or as a filling for vol-au-vents (patty shells). For a really luxurious treat, finish with ribbons of smoked salmon or prosciutto.

Put a stoned (pitted) and chopped avocado in a blender or food processor, or mash with a fork until smooth. Mix in 1 chopped spring onion (scallion), 10ml/ 2 tsp lemon juice, a dash of Worcestershire sauce, and season with salt and pepper.

Pesto

Fill hollowed-out cherry tomatoes with this basil sauce, or stir it into sour cream and spread onto warm ciabatta.
Place 3 handfuls of fresh basil leaves, 1 garlic clove, 45ml/3 tbsp freshly grated Parmesan cheese, 45ml/3 tbsp toasted pine nuts and some salt and pepper in a food processor or blender and process until well blended. With the machine running, gradually pour 60–90ml/4–6 tbsp virgin olive oil through the feeder tube until a smooth paste forms.

Tapenade

Spread tapenade on toasted ciabatta as a quick crostini, stir into soups or mix with soft (farmer's) cheese.
Process 115g/4oz/⅔ cup stoned (pitted) kalamata olives, 1–2 garlic cloves, 15ml/ 1 tbsp capers, 45ml/3 tbsp virgin olive oil, 2–4 anchovy fillets, juice of ½ lemon and 5–10ml/1–2 tsp chopped coriander (cilantro) until smooth. Season to taste.

Warm Egg & Salmon Topping

This is equally delicious served on triangles of hot buttered toast or in warm mini croissants and it is ideal for a cold winter day. Use a hotplate (burner), if you have one, to keep the food warm.

Melt a knob (pat) of butter in a small pan. Beat 2 eggs in a bowl with salt and pepper to taste. Add the eggs to the pan and cook for 2 minutes, stirring constantly. Remove from the heat and stir in 15ml/1 tbsp double (heavy) cream and 50g/2oz chopped smoked salmon. Season to taste.

Tomato & Garlic Topping

This vibrant topping is perfect served at room temperature on ciabatta bread, which will soak up all the juices. Use the freshest, juiciest tomatoes available.

Place 4 large, plum tomatoes, 2 crushed garlic cloves, a pinch of salt, grated rind and juice of ½ lemon, 1 tsp brown sugar and 30ml/2 tbsp olive oil in a pan. Cover and cook gently for 10–15 minutes or until the mixture is pulpy.

Aubergine Spread

Serve this nutty spread on toasted wholemeal (whole-wheat) bread.
Cut an aubergine (eggplant) in half lengthways and grill (broil), cut-side down, for 15–20 minutes. Leave to cool then scoop out the flesh. Put the aubergine flesh, 1 crushed garlic clove, 15ml/1 tbsp lemon juice, 30ml/2 tbsp sunflower seeds, 45ml/3 tbsp natural (plain) yogurt and a handful of fresh coriander (cilantro) in a food processor or blender and process until smooth. Season to taste.

Bagels

"The roll with a hole" is famously filled with cream cheese and lox (smoked salmon), but is equally delicious with other fillings.

Baguettes

The shape of baguettes makes them perfect for slicing and toasting under the grill (broiler). Baguettes do not keep well, so purchase on the day of use.

Ciabatta

This chewy Italian bread can be found flavoured with olives, sun-dried tomatoes, cheese and walnuts. Like the baguette, it is a popular bread to grill (broil) and serve topped with juicy, Mediterranean ingredients.

Crispbreads

Popular in Scandinavian countries, these breads are baked until they are entirely crisp and have a noticeably sweet flavour. It is best to choose a moist topping to offset their dryness.

Croissants

Made with butter, fresh croissants are undeniably luxurious. Mini croissants, available in most supermarkets, make a particularly stylish pocket for party fillings, both savoury and sweet.

Pitta Bread

Because these well-known Greek and Turkish breads form a natural pocket they are just right for stuffing.

Naan Bread

This Indian bread is light and puffy with a soft crust, and its distinctive flavour comes partly from the sour yogurt it is made with. When warm it is ideal served with a dip.

Rye Bread

The sour, earthy flavour of rye bread is the perfect accompaniment to cream cheese or cured meats. It holds its shape well, so why not try cutting out unusual shapes using a pastry cutter?

Hot Garlic & Herb Bread

Although often served as an accompaniment, garlic bread is irresistible just on its own.

Preheat the oven to 200°C/400°F/Gas 6. Make the garlic and herb butter by beating 115g/4oz/½ cup softened, unsalted butter with 5–6 large crushed garlic cloves, and 45ml/3 tbsp chopped parsley. Cut a baguette into 1cm/½in thick diagonal slices, but leave them attached at the base so that they stay intact. Spread the butter between the slices, wrap in foil and bake for 20 minutes.

Nibbles & Dips

When you are passing round the drinks, you need little snacks that are easy for guests to pick up and pop in their mouths. Little pastries, such as Duck Wontons with Spicy Mango Sauce, moreish Marinated Olives and tempting Cheese Aigrettes, fit the bill perfectly.

Marinated Olives

For the best flavour, marinate the olives for at least 5 days and serve at room temperature.

INGREDIENTS

Serves 4

225g/8oz/1⅓ cups unpitted, green olives

3 garlic cloves

5ml/1 tsp coriander seeds

2 small red chillies

2–3 thick slices of lemon, cut into pieces

1 thyme or rosemary sprig

75ml/5 tbsp white wine vinegar

1 Spread out the olives and garlic on a chopping board. Using a rolling pin, crack and flatten them slightly.

2 Crack the coriander seeds in a mortar with a pestle.

COOK'S TIP

For a change, use a mix of caraway and cumin seeds in place of the coriander.

3 Mix the olives and the garlic, coriander seeds, chillies, lemon pieces, herb sprig and white wine vinegar in a large bowl. Toss well, then transfer the mixture to a clean glass jar. Pour in enough cold water to cover. Store in the refrigerator for at least 5 days before serving at room temperature.

Salted Almonds

These crunchy salted nuts are at their best when fresh so, if you can, cook them on the day you plan to eat them.

INGREDIENTS

Serves 2–4

175g/6oz/1 cup whole almonds in their skins

15ml/1 tbsp egg white, lightly beaten

2.5ml/½ tsp coarse sea salt

COOK'S TIP

This traditional method of salt-roasting nuts gives a matt, dry-looking finish; if you want them to shine, turn the roasted nuts into a bowl, add 15ml/1 tbsp of olive oil and shake well to coat.

1 Preheat the oven to 180°C/ 350°F/Gas 4. Spread out the almonds on a baking sheet and roast for about 20 minutes, until cracked and golden.

2 Mix the egg white and salt in a bowl, add the almonds and shake well to coat.

3 Tip the almond and egg mixture on to the baking sheet, give a shake to separate the nuts, then return them to the oven for 5 minutes, until they have dried. Set aside until cold, then store in an airtight container until ready to serve.

Cheese Aigrettes

Choux pastry is often associated with sweet pastries, such as profiteroles, but these little savoury buns, flavoured with Gruyère and dusted with grated Parmesan, are just delicious. They are best made ahead and deep-fried to serve.

INGREDIENTS

Makes 30

90g/3½ oz/scant 1 cup strong plain (all-purpose) flour

2.5ml/½ tsp paprika

2.5ml/½ tsp salt

75g/3oz/6 tbsp cold butter, diced

200ml/7fl oz/scant 1 cup water

3 eggs, beaten

75g/3oz mature Gruyère cheese, grated

corn or vegetable oil, for deep-frying

50g/2oz/⅔ cup freshly grated Parmesan cheese

ground black pepper

1 Mix the flour, paprika and salt together by sifting them on to a large sheet of greaseproof (waxed) paper. Add a generous amount of ground black pepper.

2 Put the diced butter and water into a medium pan and heat gently. As soon as the butter has melted and the liquid starts to boil, quickly tip in all the seasoned flour at once and beat very hard with a wooden spoon until the dough comes away cleanly from the sides of the pan.

3 Remove the pan from the heat and cool the paste for 5 minutes. Gradually beat in enough of the beaten egg to give a stiff dropping consistency that still holds a shape on the spoon. Mix in the Gruyère.

4 Heat the oil for deep-frying to 180°C/350°F. Take a teaspoonful of the choux paste and use a second spoon to slide it into the oil. Make more aigrettes in the same way. Fry for 3–4 minutes then drain on kitchen paper and keep warm while cooking successive batches. To serve, pile the aigrettes on a warmed serving dish and sprinkle with Parmesan.

COOK'S TIP

Filling these aigrettes gives a delightful surprise as you bite through their crisp shell. Make slightly larger aigrettes by dropping a slightly larger spoonful of dough into the hot oil. Slit them open and scoop out any soft paste. Fill the centres with taramasalata or crumbled Roquefort mixed with a little fromage frais or ricotta cheese.

Parmesan Thins

These thin, crisp, savoury discs will melt in the mouth, so make plenty for guests. They are a great snack at any time of the day, so don't just keep them for parties.

INGREDIENTS

Makes 16–20

50g/2oz/½ cup plain (all-purpose) flour

40g/1½ oz/3 tbsp butter, softened

1 egg yolk

40g/1½ oz/⅔ cup freshly grated
   Parmesan cheese

pinch of salt

pinch of mustard powder

1 Rub together the flour and the butter in a bowl using your fingertips, then work in the egg yolk, Parmesan cheese, salt and mustard. Mix to bring the dough together into a ball. Shape the mixture into a log, wrap in foil or clear film (plastic wrap) and chill for 10 minutes.

2 Preheat the oven to 200°C/ 400°F/Gas 6. Cut the Parmesan log into very thin slices, 3–6mm/ ⅛–¼in maximum, and arrange on a baking sheet. Flatten with a fork to give a pretty ridged pattern. Bake for 10 minutes or until the crackers are crisp but not changing colour.

Hummus Bi Tahina

Blending chickpeas with garlic and oil creates a surprisingly creamy purée that is delicious as part of a Turkish-style mezze, or as a dip with vegetables. Leftovers make a good sandwich filler.

INGREDIENTS

Serves 4–6

150g/5oz/¾ cup dried chickpeas

juice of 2 lemons

2 garlic cloves, sliced

30ml/2 tbsp olive oil

pinch of cayenne pepper

150ml/¼ pint/⅔ cup tahini paste

salt and ground black pepper

extra olive oil and cayenne pepper,
  for sprinkling

flat leaf parsley sprigs, to garnish

1 Put the chickpeas in a bowl with plenty of cold water and leave to soak overnight.

2 Drain the chickpeas, place in a pan and cover with fresh water. Bring to the boil and boil rapidly for 10 minutes. Reduce the heat and simmer gently for about 1 hour until soft. Drain well in a colander.

3 Process the chickpeas in a food processor to a smooth purée. Add the lemon juice, garlic, olive oil, cayenne pepper and tahini paste and blend until creamy, scraping the mixture down from the sides of the bowl.

4 Season the purée with plenty of salt and ground black pepper and transfer to a serving dish. Sprinkle with a little olive oil and cayenne pepper, and serve garnished with a few parsley sprigs.

COOK'S TIP

For convenience, canned chickpeas can be used instead. Allow two 400g/14oz cans and drain them thoroughly. Tahini paste can now be purchased from most good supermarkets or health food stores.

Tzatziki

Serve this classic Greek dip with toasted small pitta breads.

INGREDIENTS

Serves 4

1 mini cucumber
4 spring onions (scallions)
1 garlic clove
200ml/7fl oz/scant 1 cup Greek
   (US strained plain) yogurt
45ml/3 tbsp chopped fresh mint
salt and ground black pepper
fresh mint sprig, to garnish (optional)

1 Trim the ends from the mini cucumber, then cut it into 5mm/¼in dice.

2 Trim the spring onions and garlic, then chop both very finely.

COOK'S TIP

Choose Greek yogurt for this dip – it has a higher fat content than most yogurts, which gives it a deliciously rich, creamy texture.

3 In a glass bowl, beat the yogurt until completely smooth, if necessary, then gently stir in the chopped cucumber, onions, garlic and mint.

4 Add salt and plenty of ground black pepper to taste. Transfer the mixture to a serving bowl. Chill until ready to serve; garnish with mint if you like.

Guacamole

Avocados discolour quickly so make this sauce just before serving. If you do need to keep it for any length of time, cover the surface of the sauce with clear film (plastic wrap) and chill in the refrigerator.

INGREDIENTS

Serves 6

2 large ripe avocados

2 red chillies, seeded

1 garlic clove

1 shallot

30ml/2 tbsp olive oil,
    plus extra to serve

juice of 1 lemon

salt and ground black pepper

flat leaf parsley leaves, to garnish

1 Halve the avocados, remove the stones (pits) and scoop out the flesh into a large bowl.

2 Using a fork or potato masher, mash the avocado flesh until smooth.

3 Finely chop the chillies, garlic and shallot, then stir into the mashed avocado with the olive oil and lemon juice. Season to taste.

4 Spoon the mixture into a small serving bowl. Drizzle over a little olive oil and sprinkle with a few flat leaf parsley leaves. Serve immediately.

Baba Ganoush with Lebanese Flatbread

Baba Ganoush is a delectable dip from the Middle East. Tahini – sesame seed paste – is the main flavouring, with cumin giving a subtle hint of spice.

INGREDIENTS

Serves 6

2 small aubergines (eggplant)
1 garlic clove, crushed
60ml/4 tbsp tahini
25g/1oz/¼ cup ground almonds
juice of ½ lemon
2.5ml/½ tsp ground cumin
30ml/2 tbsp fresh mint leaves
30ml/2 tbsp olive oil
salt and ground black pepper

For the flatbread
4 pitta breads
45ml/3 tbsp sesame seeds
45ml/3 tbsp chopped fresh thyme leaves
45ml/3 tbsp poppy seeds
150ml/¼ pint/⅔ cup olive oil

1 Start by making the Lebanese flatbread. Split the pitta breads through the middle and carefully open them out. Mix the sesame seeds, the chopped thyme and the poppy seeds in a mortar. Work them lightly with a pestle to release the flavour.

2 Stir in the oil. Spread the mixture over the cut sides of the pitta bread. Grill (broil) until golden brown. When cool, break into pieces and set aside.

3 Grill the aubergines, turning them frequently, until the skin is blackened and blistered. Remove the peel, chop the flesh roughly and leave to drain in a colander.

4 Squeeze out as much liquid from the aubergines as possible. Place the flesh in a blender or food processor, then add the garlic, tahini, ground almonds, lemon juice and cumin, with salt to taste. Process to a smooth paste, then roughly chop half the mint and stir into the dip.

5 Spoon the paste into a bowl, scatter the remaining mint leaves on top and drizzle with the olive oil. Serve with the Lebanese flatbread.

Chilli Bean Dip

*This deliciously spicy and creamy
bean dip is best served warm with
triangles of toasted pitta bread.*

INGREDIENTS

Serves 4

2 garlic cloves

1 onion

2 green chillies

30ml/2 tbsp vegetable oil

5–10ml/1–2 tsp hot chilli powder

400g/14oz can kidney beans

75g/3oz mature (sharp) Cheddar cheese,
    grated

1 red chilli, seeded

salt and ground black pepper

1 Finely chop the garlic and
onion. Seed and finely chop
the green chillies.

2 Heat the vegetable oil in a large
sauté pan or deep frying pan
and add the garlic, onion, green
chillies and chilli powder. Cook
gently for about 5 minutes, stirring
regularly, until the onions are
softened and transparent, but
not browned.

3 Drain the kidney beans,
reserving the liquor. Blend all
but 30ml/2 tbsp of the beans to a
purée in a food processor.

4 Add the puréed beans to the
pan with 30–45ml/2–3 tbsp of
the reserved liquor. Heat gently,
stirring to mix well.

5 Stir in the whole beans and
the Cheddar cheese. Cook
gently for about 2–3 minutes,
stirring until the cheese melts. Add
salt and pepper to taste.

6 Cut the red chilli into tiny
strips. Spoon the dip into 4
individual serving bowls and
sprinkle the chilli strips over the
top. Serve warm.

COOK'S TIP

For a dip with a coarser texture,
do not purée the beans; instead
mash them with a potato masher.

Lemon and Coconut Dhal Dip

A warm spicy dish, this can be served either as a dip with warmed pitta bread or as an accompaniment to cold meats.

INGREDIENTS

Serves 8

5cm/2in piece fresh root ginger

1 onion

2 garlic cloves

2 small red chillies, seeded

30ml/2 tbsp sunflower oil

5ml/1 tsp cumin seeds

150g/5oz/⅔ cup red lentils

250ml/8fl oz/1 cup water

15ml/1 tbsp hot curry paste

200ml/7fl oz/scant 1 cup coconut cream

juice of 1 lemon

handful of coriander (cilantro) leaves

25g/1oz/¼ cup flaked (sliced) almonds

salt and ground black pepper

1 Use a vegetable peeler to peel the ginger and finely chop it with the onion, garlic and chillies.

2 Heat the sunflower oil in a large, shallow pan. Add the ginger, onion, garlic, chillies and cumin seeds. Cook for about 5 minutes, until the onion is softened but not coloured.

3 Stir the lentils, water and curry paste into the pan. Bring to the boil, cover and cook gently over a low heat for about 15–20 minutes, stirring occasionally, until the lentils are just tender and not yet broken up.

4 Stir in all but 30ml/2 tbsp of the coconut cream. Bring to the boil and cook, uncovered, for a further 15–20 minutes, until the mixture is thick and pulpy. Off the heat, stir in the lemon juice and coriander leaves. Season to taste.

5 Heat a large frying pan and cook the flaked almonds for 1–2 minutes on each side until golden brown. Stir about three-quarters of the toasted almonds into the dhal.

6 Transfer the dhal to a serving bowl; swirl in the remaining coconut cream. Sprinkle over the reserved almonds, and serve.

VARIATION

Try making this dhal with yellow split peas: they take longer to cook and a little extra water has to be added but the result is equally tasty.

Basil and Lemon Dip

This lovely dip is based on fresh mayonnaise flavoured with lemon juice and two types of basil. Serve with crispy potato wedges for a delicious appetizer.

INGREDIENTS

Serves 4

2 large (US extra large) egg yolks
15ml/1 tbsp lemon juice
150ml/¼ pint/⅔ cup olive oil
150ml/¼ pint/⅔ cup sunflower oil
4 garlic cloves
handful of fresh green basil
handful of fresh opal basil
salt and ground black pepper

1 Place the egg yolks and lemon juice in a blender or food processor and process them briefly until lightly blended.

2 In a jug (pitcher), stir together the oils. With the machine running, pour in the oil very slowly, a little at a time.

3 Once half of the oil has been added, the remaining oil can be incorporated more quickly. Continue processing to form a thick, creamy mayonnaise.

4 Peel and crush the garlic cloves. Alternatively, place them on a chopping board and sprinkle with salt, then flatten them with the heel of a heavy-bladed knife and chop the flesh. Flatten the garlic again to make a coarse purée.

5 Tear both types of basil into small pieces and then stir into the mayonnaise along with the crushed garlic.

6 Add salt and pepper to taste, then transfer the dip to a serving dish. Cover and chill until ready to serve.

COOK'S TIP
~
Make sure all the ingredients are at room temperature before you start to help prevent the mixture from curdling.

Quail's Eggs with Herbs and Dips

For al fresco eating or informal entertaining, this platter of contrasting tastes and textures is delicious and certainly encourages a relaxed atmosphere. Choose the best seasonal vegetables and substitute for what is not available.

INGREDIENTS

Serves 6

1 large Italian focaccia or 2–3 Indian
    parathas or other flatbread

high quality olive oil, plus extra to serve

1 large garlic clove, finely chopped

small handful of chopped fresh mixed
    herbs, such as coriander (cilantro),
    mint, parsley and oregano

18–24 quail's eggs

30ml/2 tbsp home-made mayonnaise

30ml/2 tbsp thick sour cream

5ml/1 tsp chopped capers

5ml/1 tsp finely chopped shallot

salt and ground black pepper

225g/8oz fresh beetroot (beets), cooked in
    water or (hard) cider, peeled and sliced

½ bunch spring onions (scallions),
    trimmed and roughly chopped

60ml/4 tbsp red onion or tamarind and
    date chutney

coarse sea salt and mixed ground
    peppercorns, to serve

1 Preheat the oven to 190°C/ 375°F/Gas 5. Brush the focaccia or flatbread liberally with oil, sprinkle with garlic, your choice of herbs and seasoning and bake for 10–15 minutes, or until golden. Keep warm.

2 Put the quail's eggs into a pan of cold water, bring to the boil and boil for 4 minutes. Arrange in a serving dish. Peel the eggs if you wish or leave your guests to do their own.

3 To make the dip, combine the mayonnaise, sour cream, capers, shallot and seasoning.

4 To serve, cut the bread into wedges and serve with dishes of the quail's eggs, mayonnaise dip, beetroot, spring onion and chutney. Serve with tiny bowls of the coarse salt, ground peppercorns and olive oil for dipping.

COOK'S TIP

If you don't have time to make your own mayonnaise use the best store-bought variety available. You will probably find that you need to add less seasoning to it.

Celeriac Fritters with Mustard Dip

The combination of the hot, crispy fritters and cold mustard dip is extremely good.

INGREDIENTS

Serves 4

1 egg

115g/4oz/1½ cups ground almonds

45ml/3 tbsp freshly grated Parmesan
 cheese

45ml/3 tbsp chopped fresh parsley

1 celeriac, about 450g/1lb

lemon juice

oil, for deep-frying

salt and ground black pepper

sea salt flakes, to garnish

For the dip

150ml/¼ pint/⅔ cup sour cream

15–30ml/1–2 tbsp wholegrain mustard

1 Beat the egg well and pour into a shallow dish. Mix together the ground almonds, grated Parmesan and fresh parsley in a separate dish. Season with salt and plenty of ground black pepper. Set aside.

2 Peel and cut the celeriac into batons about 1cm/½in wide and 5cm/2in long. Drop them immediately into a bowl of water with a little lemon juice added to prevent discoloration.

3 Heat the oil to 180°C/350°F. Drain and then pat dry half the celeriac batons. Dip them into the beaten egg, then into the ground almond mixture, making sure that the pieces are coated completely and evenly.

4 Deep-fry the fritters, in batches, for 2–3 minutes until golden. Drain on kitchen paper. Keep warm while you cook the remaining fritters.

5 Make the dip. Mix the sour cream, mustard and salt to taste. Spoon into a serving bowl. Sprinkle the fritters with sea salt.

Duck Wontons with Spicy Mango Sauce

These Chinese-style wontons are easy to make using ready-cooked smoked duck or chicken, or even leftovers from the Sunday roast.

Makes about 40

15ml/1 tbsp light soy sauce

5ml/1 tsp sesame oil

2 spring onions (scallions), finely chopped

grated rind of ½ orange

5ml/1 tsp soft light brown sugar

275g/10oz/1½ cups chopped smoked duck

about 40 small wonton wrappers

15ml/1 tbsp vegetable oil

whole fresh chives, to garnish (optional)

For the mango sauce

30ml/2 tbsp vegetable oil

5ml/1 tsp ground cumin

2.5ml/½ tsp ground cardamom

1.5ml/¼ tsp ground cinnamon

250ml/8fl oz/1 cup mango purée (about 1 large mango)

15ml/1 tbsp clear honey

2.5ml/½ tsp Chinese chilli sauce (or to taste)

15ml/1 tbsp cider vinegar

chopped fresh chives, to garnish

1 First prepare the sauce. In a medium pan, heat the oil over a medium-low heat. Add the ground cumin, cardamom and cinnamon and cook for about 3 minutes, stirring constantly.

2 Stir in the mango purée, honey, chilli sauce and vinegar. Remove from the heat and leave to cool. Pour into a bowl and cover until ready to serve.

3 Prepare the wonton filling. In a large bowl, mix together the soy sauce, sesame oil, spring onions, orange rind and brown sugar until well blended. Add the duck and toss to coat well.

4 Place a teaspoonful of the duck mixture in the centre of each wonton wrapper. Brush the edges with water and then draw them up to the centre, twisting to seal and forming a pouch shape.

5 Preheat the oven to 190°F/ 375°C/Gas 5. Line a large baking sheet with foil and brush lightly with oil. Arrange the wontons on the baking sheet and bake for 10–12 minutes until crisp and golden. Serve with the mango sauce garnished with chopped fresh chives. If you wish, tie each wonton with a fresh chive.

COOK'S TIP

Wonton wrappers, available in some large supermarkets and Asian food stores, are sold in 450g/1lb packets and can be stored in the freezer almost indefinitely. Remove as many as you need, keeping the rest frozen.

Pork and Peanut Wontons with Plum Sauce

The wontons can be filled and set aside up to 8 hours before cooking.

INGREDIENTS

Makes 40–50 wontons

175g/6oz/1½ cups minced (ground) pork
  or 175g/6oz pork sausages, skinned
  (casings removed)
2 spring onions (scallions),
  finely chopped
30ml/2 tbsp peanut butter
10ml/2 tsp oyster sauce (optional)
40–50 wonton skins
30ml/2 tbsp equal mixture of flour
  and water
vegetable oil, for deep-frying
salt and ground black pepper
lettuces and radishes, to garnish

For the plum sauce
225g/8oz/generous ¾ cup dark plum jam
15ml/1 tbsp rice or white wine vinegar
15ml/1 tbsp dark soy sauce
2.5ml/½ tsp chilli sauce

1 Combine the minced pork or
skinned sausages, spring
onions, peanut butter, oyster sauce,
if using, and seasoning, and then
set aside.

2 For the plum sauce, combine
the plum jam, vinegar, soy and
chilli sauces in a serving bowl and
set aside.

3 To fill the wonton skins, place
8 wrappers at a time on a work
surface, moisten the edges with the
flour paste and place 2.5ml/½ tsp
of the filling on each one. Fold in
half, corner to corner, and twist.

4 Fill a wok or deep frying pan
one-third with vegetable oil
and heat to 190°C/375°F. Have
ready a wire strainer or frying
basket and a tray lined with
kitchen paper. Drop the wontons,
8 at a time, into the hot fat and
fry until golden all over, for about
1–2 minutes. Lift out on to the
paper-lined tray and sprinkle with
fine salt. Serve with the plum sauce
garnished with lettuce and radishes.

Vegetable Tempura

Tempura is a Japanese type of savoury fritter. Originally prawns were used, but vegetables can be cooked in the egg batter successfully too. The secret of making the incredibly light batter is to use really cold water, and to have the oil at the right temperature before you start cooking the fritters.

INGREDIENTS

Serves 4

2 courgettes (zucchini)
$\frac{1}{2}$ aubergine (eggplant)
1 large carrot
$\frac{1}{2}$ small Spanish onion
1 egg
120ml/4fl oz/$\frac{1}{2}$ cup iced water
115g/4oz/1 cup plain (all-purpose) flour
salt and ground black pepper
vegetable oil, for deep-frying
sea salt flakes, lemon slices and Japanese
   soy sauce (*shoyu*), to serve

1 Using a potato peeler, pare strips of peel from the courgettes and aubergine to give a striped effect.

2 Using a chef's knife, cut the courgettes, aubergine and carrot into strips measuring about 7.5–10cm/3–4in long and 3mm/$\frac{1}{8}$in wide. Place in a colander and sprinkle with salt. Put a small plate on top and weight it down. Leave for 30 minutes, rinse thoroughly, and dry with kitchen paper.

3 Thinly slice the onion from top to base, discarding the plump pieces in the middle. Separate the layers so that there are lots of fine, long strips. Mix all the vegetables together and season with salt and pepper.

4 Make the batter immediately before frying. Mix the egg and iced water in a bowl, then sift in the flour. Mix briefly with a fork or chopsticks. Do not overmix: the batter should remain lumpy. Add the vegetables to the batter and mix to combine.

5 Half-fill a wok with oil and heat to 180°C/350°F. Scoop up a heaped tablespoonful of the mixture at a time and carefully lower it into the oil. Deep-fry in batches for about 3 minutes, until golden brown and crisp. Drain on kitchen paper.

6 Serve each portion with salt, slices of lemon and a tiny bowl of Japanese soy sauce for dipping.

> ### COOK'S TIP
> ❧
> Other suitable vegetables for tempura include mushrooms and slices of red, green, yellow or orange (bell) peppers.

Things on Sticks

Skewers and sticks hold delicious ingredients together in easy-to-manage pieces that can be prepared in advance, ready for a quick grilling, to be served with delicious sauces. From Tandoori Chicken Sticks to Potato Skewers with Mustard Dip, the varieties here will please everyone.

Potato Skewers with Mustard Dip

Potatoes cooked on the barbecue have a great flavour and crisp skin. Try these delicious kebabs served with a thick, garlic-rich dip for an unusual start to a meal.

INGREDIENTS

Serves 6

For the dip

4 garlic cloves, crushed

2 egg yolks

30ml/2 tbsp lemon juice

300ml/½ pint/1¼ cups extra virgin olive oil

10ml/2 tsp wholegrain mustard

salt and ground black pepper

For the skewers

1kg/2¼ lb small new potatoes

200g/7oz shallots, halved

30ml/2 tbsp olive oil

15ml/1 tbsp sea salt

1 Prepare the barbecue or preheat the grill (broiler). To make the dip place the garlic, egg yolks and lemon juice in a blender or a food processor and process for just a few seconds until the mixture is smooth.

2 Keep the blender motor running and add the oil very gradually, pouring it in a thin stream, until the mixture forms a thick, glossy cream. Add the mustard and stir the ingredients together, then season with salt and pepper. Chill until ready to use.

3 Par-boil the potatoes in their skins in boiling water for 5 minutes. Drain well and then thread them on to metal skewers, alternating with the shallots.

4 Brush the skewers with oil and sprinkle with salt. Cook on the barbecue or grill (broil) for about 10–12 minutes, turning occasionally. Serve with the dip.

COOK'S TIP

Only early or "new" potatoes and salad potatoes have the firmness necessary to stay on the skewer.

Aromatic Tiger Prawns

There is no elegant way to eat these aromatic prawns – just hold them by the tails, pull them off the sticks with your fingers and pop them into your mouth.

INGREDIENTS

Serves 4

16 raw tiger prawns (jumbo shrimp)

2.5ml/½ tsp chilli powder

5ml/1 tsp fennel seeds

5 Sichuan or black peppercorns

1 star anise, broken into segments

1 cinnamon stick, broken into pieces

30ml/2 tbsp groundnut (peanut) oil

2 garlic cloves, chopped

2cm/¾in piece fresh root ginger, peeled and finely chopped

1 shallot, chopped

30ml/2 tbsp water

30ml/2 tbsp rice vinegar

30ml/2 tbsp soft light brown sugar

salt and ground black pepper

lime slices and chopped spring onion (scallion), to garnish

1 Thread the prawns in pairs on to 8 wooden cocktail sticks (toothpicks). Set aside. Heat a frying pan, put in the chilli powder, fennel seeds, Sichuan or black peppercorns, star anise and cinnamon stick and dry-fry for 1–2 minutes to release the flavours. Leave to cool, then grind coarsely in a grinder or tip into a mortar and crush with a pestle.

2 Heat the groundnut oil in a shallow pan, add the garlic, ginger and chopped shallot and then fry gently until very lightly coloured. Add the crushed spices and seasoning and cook the mixture gently for 2 minutes. Pour in the water and simmer, stirring, for 5 minutes.

3 Add the rice vinegar and soft brown sugar, stir until dissolved, then add the prawns. Cook for about 3–5 minutes, until the shellfish have turned pink, but are still very juicy. Serve hot, garnished with lime slices and spring onion.

COOK'S TIP

~

If you buy whole prawns, remove the heads before cooking them.

King Prawns with Spicy Dip

The spicy dip served with this dish is equally good made from peanuts instead of cashew nuts.

Serves 4–6

24 raw king prawns (jumbo shrimp)
juice of ½ lemon
5ml/1 tsp paprika
1 bay leaf
1 thyme sprig
vegetable oil, for brushing
salt and ground black pepper

For the spicy dip

1 onion, chopped
4 canned plum tomatoes, plus 60ml/4 tbsp
   of the juice
½ green (bell) pepper, seeded
   and chopped
1 garlic clove, crushed
15ml/1 tbsp cashew nuts
15ml/1 tbsp soy sauce
15ml/1 tbsp desiccated (dry, unsweetened
   shredded) coconut

1 Peel the prawns, if necessary, leaving the tails on. Place in a shallow dish and sprinkle with the lemon juice, paprika and seasoning. Cover and chill.

2 Put the shells in a pan with the bay leaf and thyme, cover with water, and bring to the boil. Simmer for 30 minutes; strain the stock into a measuring jug (cup). Top up with water, if necessary, to 300ml/½ pint/1¼ cups.

3 To make the spicy dip, place all the ingredients in a blender or food processor and process until the mixture is smooth.

4 Pour into a pan with the prawn stock and simmer over a moderate heat for 30 minutes, until the sauce is fairly thick.

5 Preheat the grill (broiler). Thread the prawns on to small skewers, then brush the prawns on both sides with a little oil and grill (broil) under a low heat until cooked, turning once. Serve with the dip.

COOK'S TIP

If unshelled raw prawns are not available, use cooked king prawns instead. Just grill them for a short time, until they are completely heated through.

Italian Prawn Skewers

Parsley and lemon are all that is required to create a lovely tiger prawn dish. Grill them, or cook on a barbecue for an informal al fresco summer appetizer.

INGREDIENTS

Serves 4

900g/2lb raw tiger prawns (jumbo shrimp), peeled
60ml/4 tbsp olive oil
45ml/3 tbsp vegetable oil
75g/3oz/1¼ cups fine dry breadcrumbs
1 garlic clove, crushed
15ml/1 tbsp chopped fresh parsley
salt and ground black pepper
lemon wedges, to serve

1 Slit the prawns down their backs and remove the dark vein. Rinse in cold water and pat dry on kitchen paper.

2 Put the olive oil and vegetable oil in a large bowl and add the tiger prawns, mixing them to coat evenly. Add the breadcrumbs, garlic and parsley and season with salt and pepper. Toss the prawns thoroughly, to give them an even coating of breadcrumbs. Cover and leave to marinate for about 1 hour.

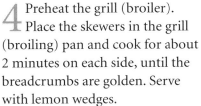

4 Preheat the grill (broiler). Place the skewers in the grill (broiling) pan and cook for about 2 minutes on each side, until the breadcrumbs are golden. Serve with lemon wedges.

3 Thread the prawns on to 4 metal or wooden skewers, curling them up as you work, so that the tails are skewered neatly in the middle.

Scallop and Mussel Kebabs

These delightfully crispy shellfish skewers are served with hot toast spread with a lovely fresh herb butter.

INGREDIENTS

Serves 4

65g/2½oz/5 tbsp butter, at room
   temperature
30ml/2 tbsp minced (ground) fresh fennel
   or parsley
15ml/1 tbsp lemon juice
32 small scallops
24 large mussels, in the shell
8 bacon rashers (strips)
50g/2oz/1 cup fresh breadcrumbs
50ml/2fl oz/¼ cup olive oil
salt and ground black pepper
hot toast, to serve

1 Make the flavoured butter by combining the butter with the minced herbs and lemon juice. Add salt and pepper to taste. Mix well and set aside.

2 In a small pan, cook the scallops in their own liquor until they begin to shrink. (If there is no scallop liquor – retained from the shells after shucking – use a little fish stock or white wine.) Drain the scallops well and then pat dry with kitchen paper.

3 Scrub the mussels well and remove their beards, then rinse under cold running water. Place in a large pan with about 2.5cm/1in of water in the base. Cover and steam the mussels over a medium heat until they open. When cool enough to handle, remove them from their shells, and pat dry using kitchen paper. Discard any mussels that have not opened during cooking.

4 Take 8 15cm/6in wooden or metal skewers. Thread on each one, alternately, 4 scallops and 3 mussels. As you are doing this, weave a rasher of bacon between the scallops and mussels.

5 Preheat the grill (broiler). Spread the breadcrumbs on a plate. Brush the shellfish with oil and roll in the crumbs to coat.

6 Place the skewers on the grill rack. Grill (broil) until crisp and browned, 4–5 minutes on each side. Serve immediately with hot toast and the flavoured butter.

Salmon and Scallop Brochettes

With their delicate colours and superb flavour, these skewers make the perfect opener for a sophisticated party.

INGREDIENTS

Serves 4

8 lemon grass stalks

225g/8oz salmon fillet, skinned

8 shucked queen scallops, with their corals if possible

8 baby (pearl) onions, peeled and blanched

½ yellow (bell) pepper, cut into 8 squares

25g/1oz/2 tbsp butter

juice of ½ lemon

salt, ground white pepper and paprika

For the sauce

30ml/2 tbsp dry vermouth

50g/2oz/¼ cup butter

5ml/1 tsp chopped fresh tarragon

1 Preheat the grill (broiler) to medium-high. Cut off the top 7.5–10cm/3–4in of each lemon grass stalk. Reserve the bulb ends for another dish. Cut the salmon fillet into 12 2cm/¾ in cubes. Thread the salmon, scallops, corals if available, onions and pepper squares on to the lemon grass and arrange the brochettes in a grill (broiling) pan.

2 Melt the butter in a small pan, add the lemon juice and a pinch of paprika and then brush all over the brochettes. Grill (broil) the skewers for about 2–3 minutes on each side, turning and basting the brochettes every minute, until the fish and scallops are just cooked, but are still very juicy. Transfer to a platter and keep hot while you make the sauce.

3 Pour the dry vermouth and the leftover cooking juices from the brochettes into a small pan and boil fiercely to reduce by half. Add the butter and melt, then stir in the chopped fresh tarragon and salt and ground white pepper to taste. Pour the tarragon butter sauce over the brochettes and serve.

Sushi-style Tuna Cubes

These tasty tuna cubes are easier to prepare than classic Japanese sushi but retain the same fresh taste.

INGREDIENTS

Makes about 24

675g/1½ lb fresh tuna steak, about 2cm/¾ in thick

1 large red (bell) pepper, seeded and cut into 2cm/¾ in pieces

sesame seeds, for sprinkling

For the marinade

15–30ml/1–2 tbsp lemon juice

2.5ml/½ tsp salt

2.5ml/½ tsp sugar

2.5ml/½ tsp wasabi paste

120ml/4 fl oz/½ cup olive or vegetable oil

30ml/2 tbsp chopped coriander (cilantro)

For the soy dipping sauce

105ml/7 tbsp soy sauce

15ml/1 tbsp rice wine vinegar

5ml/1 tsp lemon juice

1–2 spring onions (scallions), finely chopped

5ml/1 tsp caster (superfine) sugar

2–3 dashes hot pepper sauce

1 Cut the tuna into 2.5cm/1in pieces and then arrange them in a single layer in a large non-corrosive baking dish.

2 Prepare the marinade. In a small bowl, stir the lemon juice with the salt, sugar and wasabi paste. Slowly whisk in the oil until well blended and slightly creamy. Stir in the coriander. Pour over the tuna cubes and toss to coat. Cover and marinate for about 40 minutes in a cool place.

3 Meanwhile, prepare the soy dipping sauce. Combine all the ingredients in a small bowl and stir until well blended. Cover until ready to serve.

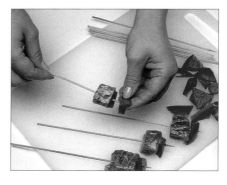

4 Preheat the grill (broiler) and line a baking sheet with foil. Thread a cube of tuna then a piece of pepper on to each skewer and arrange on the baking sheet.

5 Sprinkle with sesame seeds and grill (broil) for 3–5 minutes, turning once or twice, until just beginning to colour but still pink inside. Serve with the soy dipping sauce.

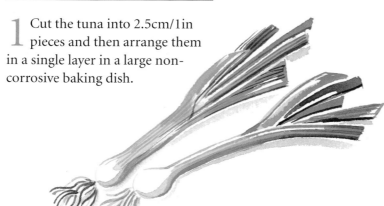

COOK'S TIP

Wasabi is a hot, pungent Japanese horseradish available in powder form (that has to be reconstituted) and as paste in a tube from gourmet and Japanese food stores.

Chicken Satay with Peanut Sauce

These skewers of marinated chicken can be prepared in advance and served at room temperature. Beef, pork or even lamb fillet can be used instead of chicken if you prefer.

INGREDIENTS

Makes about 24

450g/1lb skinless, boneless, chicken
   breast portions
oil, for brushing
sesame seeds, for sprinkling
red (bell) pepper strips, to garnish

For the marinade

90ml/6 tbsp vegetable oil
60ml/4 tbsp tamari or light soy sauce
60ml/4 tbsp fresh lime juice
2.5cm/1in piece fresh root ginger, peeled
   and chopped
3–4 garlic cloves
30ml/2 tbsp soft light brown sugar
5ml/1 tsp Chinese-style chilli sauce or
   1 small red chilli pepper, seeded
   and chopped
30ml/2 tbsp chopped coriander (cilantro)

For the peanut sauce

30ml/2 tbsp smooth peanut butter
30ml/2 tbsp soy sauce
15ml/1 tbsp sesame or vegetable oil
2 spring onions (scallions), chopped
2 garlic cloves
15–30ml/1–2 tbsp fresh lime or
   lemon juice
15ml/1 tbsp soft light brown sugar

COOK'S TIP

When using metal skewers, look for flat ones, which prevent the food from spinning around. If using wooden skewers, be sure to soak them in cold water for at least 30 minutes, to prevent them from burning.

1 Prepare the marinade. Place all the marinade ingredients in a food processor or blender and process until smooth and well blended, scraping down the sides of the bowl once. Pour into a shallow dish and set aside.

2 Into the same food processor or blender, put all the peanut sauce ingredients and process until well blended. If the sauce is too thick, add a little water and process again. Pour into a small bowl and cover until ready to serve.

3 Slice the chicken portions into thin strips, then cut the strips into 2cm/ ¾in pieces.

4 Add the chicken pieces to the marinade in the dish. Toss well to coat, cover and marinate for about 3–4 hours in a cool place, or overnight in the refrigerator.

5 Preheat the grill (broiler). Line a baking sheet with foil and brush lightly with oil. Thread 2–3 pieces of marinated chicken on to skewers and sprinkle with the sesame seeds. Grill (broil) for 4–5 minutes until golden, turning once. Serve with the peanut sauce, and a garnish of red pepper strips.

Tandoori Chicken Sticks

This aromatic chicken dish is traditionally baked in a special clay oven called a tandoor.

INGREDIENTS

Makes about 25

450g/1lb skinless, boneless chicken
   breast portions

For the coriander yogurt dip

250ml/8fl oz/1 cup natural (plain) yogurt

30ml/2 tbsp whipping cream

½ cucumber, peeled, seeded and
   finely chopped

15–30ml/1–2 tbsp fresh chopped mint
   or coriander (cilantro)

salt and ground black pepper

For the marinade

175ml/6fl oz/¾ cup natural (plain) yogurt

5ml/1 tsp garam masala or curry powder

1.5ml/¼ tsp ground cumin

1.5ml/¼ tsp ground coriander

1.5ml/¼ tsp cayenne pepper (or to taste)

5ml/1 tsp tomato purée (paste)

1–2 garlic cloves, finely chopped

2.5cm/1in piece fresh root ginger, peeled
   and finely chopped

grated rind and juice of
   ½ lemon

15–30ml/1–2 tbsp chopped fresh mint
   or coriander (cilantro)

1 Prepare the coriander yogurt. Combine all the ingredients in a bowl and season with salt and ground black pepper. Cover with clear film (plastic wrap) and chill until you are ready to serve.

2 Prepare the marinade. Place all the ingredients in the bowl of a food processor, and process until the mixture is smooth. Pour into a shallow dish.

3 Freeze the chicken portions for 5 minutes to firm, then slice in half horizontally. Cut the slices into 2cm/¾in strips and add to the marinade. Toss to coat well. Cover and chill in the refrigerator for 6–8 hours or overnight.

4 Preheat the grill (broiler) and line a baking sheet with foil. Using a slotted spoon, remove the chicken from the marinade and arrange the pieces in a single layer on the baking sheet. Scrunch up the chicken slightly so it makes wavy shapes. Grill (broil) for 4–5 minutes until brown and just cooked, turning once. When cool enough to handle, thread 1–2 pieces on to cocktail sticks or short skewers and serve with the dip.

Skewered Lamb with Red Onion Salsa

This summery tapas dish is ideal for outdoor eating, although, if the weather fails, the skewers can be cooked in the oven rather than on a barbecue. The simple salsa makes a refreshing accompaniment – make sure that you use a mild-flavoured red onion that is fresh and crisp, and a ripe, flavourful tomato.

INGREDIENTS

Serves 4

225g/8oz lean lamb, cubed
2.5ml/½ tsp ground cumin
5ml/1 tsp paprika
15ml/1 tbsp olive oil
salt and ground black pepper

For the salsa

1 red onion, very thinly sliced
1 large tomato, seeded and chopped
15ml/1 tbsp red wine vinegar
3–4 fresh basil or mint leaves,
    coarsely torn
small mint leaves, to garnish

1 Place the lamb in a bowl with the cumin, paprika, olive oil and plenty of salt and pepper. Toss well until the lamb is coated with spices.

2 Cover the bowl with clear film (plastic wrap) and set aside in a cool place for a few hours, or in the refrigerator overnight, so that the lamb absorbs the flavours.

3 Spear the lamb cubes on 4 small skewers – if using wooden skewers, soak first in cold water for 30 minutes to prevent them from burning.

4 To make the salsa, put the sliced onion, tomato, red wine vinegar and basil or mint leaves in a small bowl and stir together until thoroughly blended. Season to taste with salt, garnish with mint, then set aside while you cook the lamb skewers.

5 Cook over the barbecue or under a preheated grill (broiler) for 5–10 minutes, turning frequently, until the lamb is well browned but still slightly pink in the centre. Serve with the salsa.

Lamb Tikka

Creamy yogurt and ground nuts go wonderfully with the spices in these little Indian meatballs.

INGREDIENTS

Makes about 20
450g/1lb lamb fillet
2 spring onions (scallions), chopped

For the marinade
350ml/12 fl oz/1½ cups natural
    (plain) yogurt
15ml/1 tbsp ground almonds or peanuts
15ml/1 tbsp vegetable oil
2–3 garlic cloves, finely chopped
juice of 1 lemon
5ml/1 tsp garam masala or curry powder
2.5ml/½ tsp ground cardamom
1.5ml/¼ tsp cayenne pepper
15–30ml/1–2 tbsp chopped fresh mint

2 Cut the lamb into small pieces and put in the bowl of a food processor with the spring onions. Process, using the pulse action, until the meat is finely chopped. Add 30–45ml/2–3 tbsp of the marinade and process again.

4 With moistened palms, form the meat mixture into slightly oval-shaped balls, measuring about 4cm/1½in long, and arrange in a shallow baking dish. Spoon over the remaining marinade and chill the meatballs for 8–10 hours or overnight.

3 Test to see if the mixture holds together by pinching a little between your fingertips. Add a little more marinade if necessary, but do not make the mixture too wet and soft.

1 Stir together the marinade ingredients. In a separate small bowl, reserve about 120ml/4fl oz/½ cup of the mixture to use as a dipping sauce for the meatballs.

5 Preheat the grill (broiler) and line a baking sheet with foil. Thread each meatball on to a skewer and arrange on the baking sheet. Grill (broil) for 4–5 minutes, turning them occasionally, until crisp and golden on all sides. Serve with the reserved marinade as a dipping sauce.

Pork Satay

*Originating in Indonesia, satay are
skewers of meat marinated with
spices and grilled quickly over
charcoal. It's street food at its best,
prepared by vendors with portable
grills who set up stalls at every road
side and market place. It makes a
great-tasting appetizer too. It's not
too filling and it's bursting with
flavour. You can make satay with
chicken, beef or lamb. Serve with
satay sauce, and a cucumber relish if
you like.*

INGREDIENTS

Makes about 20
450g/1lb lean pork
5ml/1 tsp grated fresh root ginger
1 lemon grass stalk, finely
    chopped
3 garlic cloves, finely chopped
15ml/1 tbsp medium curry paste
5ml/1 tsp ground cumin
5ml/1 tsp ground turmeric
60ml/4 tbsp coconut cream
30ml/2 tbsp fish sauce
5ml/1 tsp granulated sugar
oil, for brushing
fresh herbs, to garnish

For the satay sauce
250ml/8fl oz/1 cup coconut milk
30ml/2 tbsp red curry paste
75g/3oz crunchy peanut butter
120ml/4fl oz/$^1\!/_2$ cup chicken stock
45ml/3 tbsp soft light brown sugar
30ml/2 tbsp tamarind juice
15ml/1 tbsp fish sauce
2.5ml/$^1\!/_2$ tsp salt

1 Cut the pork thinly into
5cm/2in strips. Mix together
the fresh root ginger, lemon grass,
garlic, curry paste, cumin,
turmeric, coconut cream, fish
sauce and sugar.

2 Pour over the pork and leave
to marinate for about 2 hours.

3 Meanwhile, make the sauce.
Heat the coconut milk over a
medium heat, then add the red
curry paste, peanut butter, chicken
stock and sugar.

4 Cook and stir until smooth,
about 5–6 minutes. Add the
tamarind juice, fish sauce and salt
to taste.

5 Thread the meat on to
skewers. Brush with oil and
grill over charcoal or under a
preheated grill (broiler) for 3–4
minutes on each side, turning
occasionally, until cooked and
golden brown. Serve with the satay
sauce, garnished with fresh herbs.

Beef Satay with a Hot Mango Dip

Tender beef is flavoured with a spicy marinade before being grilled then served with a fruit dip.

INGREDIENTS

Makes 12 skewers

450g/1lb sirloin steak,
  2cm/¾ in thick, trimmed

For the marinade

15ml/1 tbsp coriander seeds
5ml/1 tsp cumin seeds
50g/2oz/⅓ cup raw cashew nuts
15ml/1 tbsp vegetable oil
2 shallots, or 1 small onion, finely chopped
1cm/½in piece fresh root ginger, peeled
  and finely chopped
1 garlic clove, crushed
30ml/2 tbsp tamarind sauce
30ml/2 tbsp dark soy sauce
10ml/2 tsp sugar
5ml/1 tsp rice or white wine vinegar

For the mango dip

1 ripe mango
1–2 small red chillies, seeded and
  finely chopped
15ml/1 tbsp fish sauce
juice of 1 lime
10ml/2 tsp caster (superfine) sugar
1.5ml/¼ tsp salt
30ml/2 tbsp chopped fresh
  coriander (cilantro)

1 Soak 12 wooden skewers for 30 minutes. Slice the beef into long narrow strips and thread, zigzag-style, on to the skewers. Lay on a flat plate and set aside.

2 For the marinade, dry-fry the seeds and nuts in a large wok until evenly brown. Transfer to a mortar with a rough surface and crush finely with the pestle. Add the oil, shallots or onion, ginger, garlic, tamarind and soy sauces, sugar and rice or white wine vinegar.

3 Spread this marinade over the beef and leave to marinate for up to 8 hours. Cook the beef under a moderate grill (broiler) or over a barbecue for 6–8 minutes, turning to ensure an even colour. Meanwhile, make the mango dip.

4 Cut away the skin and remove the stone (pit) from the mango. Process the mango flesh with the chillies, fish sauce, lime juice, sugar and salt until smooth, then add the coriander.

Finger Food

From Tuna in Rolled Red Peppers to Potato Blinis, you can wrap or top all kinds of delicious ingredients with others. Besides making a perfect bitesize snack, these dishes are neat to eat and require only a napkin, saving on later dishwashing.

Assorted Canapés

These elegant party pieces take a little time to make, but they can be prepared in advance with the final touches added when your guests arrive. Each variation makes 12.

TRUFFLE CANAPÉS

INGREDIENTS

225/8oz rich shortcrust
  (unsweetened) pastry
2 eggs, beaten
15g/½oz/1 tbsp butter
5ml/1 tsp truffle oil or a few slices or
  shreds of fresh truffle
salt and ground black pepper
chopped chives, to garnish

1 Preheat the oven to 190°C/
375°F/Gas 5. Roll out the pastry very thinly on a lightly floured work surface and use to line 12 very small tartlet tins (muffin pans).

2 Line the base of each pastry case (shell) with baking parchment and bake for 10 minutes. Remove the parchment and bake for a further 5 minutes until the pastry is crisp and golden.

3 Season the beaten eggs, then melt the butter in a pan, pour in the eggs and stir constantly over a gentle heat. When the eggs are almost set, stir in the truffle oil or fresh truffle. Spoon the mixture into the pastry cases and top with chives.

PRAWN & TOMATO CANAPÉS

INGREDIENTS

225g/8oz rich shortcrust
  (unsweetened) pastry
2 tomatoes, skinned, seeded and chopped
12 large cooked prawns (shrimp), peeled
  but tails left on
60ml/4 tbsp hollandaise sauce
salt and ground black pepper
fennel or chervil sprigs, to garnish

1 Preheat the oven to 190°C/
375°F/Gas 5. Roll out the pastry very thinly on a lightly floured work surface and use to line 12 very small tartlet tins (muffin pans).

2 Line the base of each pastry case (shell) with baking parchment and bake for about 10 minutes. Remove the parchment and bake for a further 5 minutes until the pastry is crisp and golden.

3 Place some chopped tomato in the base of each pastry case and season with salt and ground black pepper. Top with the prawns and spoon on some hollandaise sauce. Warm through briefly in the oven and serve garnished with fennel or chervil sprigs.

SALMON & CORIANDER CANAPÉS

INGREDIENTS

3–4 slices dark rye bread
2 eggs, hard-boiled (hard-cooked) and
  thinly sliced
115g/4oz poached salmon
few fresh coriander (cilantro) leaves,
  to garnish

For the lime and coriander mayonnaise
45–60ml/3–4 tbsp mayonnaise
5ml/1 tsp chopped fresh
  coriander (cilantro)
5ml/1 tsp lime juice
salt and ground black pepper

1 Cut the rye bread into 12 triangular pieces, using a sharp knife.

2 Make the lime and coriander mayonnaise. In a small bowl, mix together the mayonnaise, chopped coriander and lime juice. Season with salt and ground black pepper to taste.

3 Top each bread triangle with a slice of egg, a small portion of salmon and a teaspoon of mayonnaise. Garnish each with a coriander leaf. Chill the canapés until ready to serve.

WATERCRESS & AVOCADO
CANAPÉS

INGREDIENTS

3–4 slices dark rye bread

1 small ripe avocado

15ml/1 tbsp lemon juice

45ml/3 tbsp mayonnaise

½ bunch watercress, chopped, reserving
   a few sprigs to garnish

6 quail's eggs, hard-boiled (hard-cooked)

1 Cut the bread into 12 rounds, using a plain or fluted biscuit (cookie) cutter.

2 Cut the avocado in half, around the stone (pit). Peel one half, then slice and dip each piece in lemon juice. Place one piece of avocado on each bread round.

3 Scoop the remaining avocado into a bowl and mash. Mix in the mayonnaise and watercress. Spoon a little of the mixture on to each canapé, top with a peeled, halved quail's egg and garnish with a sprig of watercress.

Mini Baked Potatoes with Blue Cheese

These miniature potatoes can be eaten with the fingers. They provide a great way of starting off an informal supper party.

INGREDIENTS

Makes 20

20 small new or salad potatoes

60ml/4 tbsp vegetable oil

coarse salt

120ml/4fl oz/½ cup sour cream

25g/1oz blue cheese, crumbled

30ml/2 tbsp chopped fresh chives,
   to garnish

1 Preheat the oven to 180°C/ 350°F/Gas 4. Wash and dry the potatoes. Toss with the oil in a bowl to coat.

2 Dip the potatoes in the coarse salt to coat lightly. Spread the potatoes out on a baking sheet. Bake for 45–50 minutes until the potatoes are tender.

3 In a small bowl, combine the sour cream and blue cheese, mixing together well.

COOK'S TIP

This dish works just as well as a light snack; if you don't want to be bothered with lots of fiddly small potatoes, simply bake an ordinary baking potato.

4 Cut a cross in the top of each potato. Press gently with your fingers to open the potatoes.

5 Top each potato with a dollop of the blue cheese mixture. Place on a serving dish and garnish with the chives. Serve hot or at room temperature.

Samosas

These tasty party snacks are enjoyed the world over. Throughout the East, they are sold by street vendors, and eaten at any time of day. Filo pastry can be used if a lighter, flakier texture is preferred.

Makes about 20

1 packet 25cm/10in square spring roll (egg roll) wrappers, thawed if frozen
30ml/2 tbsp plain (all-purpose) flour, mixed to a paste with water
vegetable oil, for deep-frying
coriander (cilantro) leaves, to garnish

For the filling

25g/1oz/2 tbsp ghee or unsalted butter
1 small onion, finely chopped
1cm/½in piece fresh root ginger, peeled and chopped
1 garlic glove, crushed
2.5ml/½ tsp chilli powder
1 large potato, about 225g/8oz, cooked until just tender and finely diced
50g/2oz/½ cup cauliflower florets, lightly cooked, chopped into small pieces
50g/2oz/½ cup frozen peas, thawed
5–10ml/1–2 tsp garam masala
15ml/1 tbsp chopped coriander (cilantro), leaves and stems
squeeze of lemon juice
salt

1 Heat the ghee or butter in a large frying pan and fry the onion, ginger and garlic for 5 minutes until the onion has softened but not browned. Add the chilli powder and cook for 1 minute, then stir in the potato, cauliflower and peas. Sprinkle with garam masala and set aside to cool. Stir in the chopped coriander, lemon juice and salt.

2 Cut the spring roll wrappers into 3 strips (or 2 for larger samosas). Brush the edges with a little of the flour paste. Place a small spoonful of filling about 2cm/¾in in from the edge of one strip. Fold one corner over the filling to make a triangle and continue this folding until the entire strip has been used and a triangular pastry has been formed. Seal any open edges with more flour and water paste, if necessary adding more water if the paste is very thick.

3 Heat the oil for deep-frying to 190°C/375°F and fry the samosas, a few at a time, until golden and crisp. Drain well on kitchen paper and serve hot, garnished with coriander leaves.

COOK'S TIP

Prepare samosas in advance by frying until just cooked through and then draining. Cook in hot oil for a few minutes to brown and drain again before serving.

Pickled Quail's Eggs

These Chinese eggs are pickled in alcohol and can be stored in a preserving jar in a cool dark place for several months. They will make delicious bitesize snacks at a drinks party and are sure to delight guests.

INGREDIENTS

Serves 12

12 quail's eggs

15ml/1 tbsp salt

750ml/1¼ pints/3 cups distilled or previously boiled water

15ml/1 tsp Sichuan peppercorns

150ml/¼ pint/⅔ cup spirit such as Mou-tal (Chinese brandy), brandy, whisky, rum or vodka

dipping sauce (see Cook's Tip) and toasted sesame seeds, to serve

1 Boil the eggs for about 3 minutes until the yolks are soft but not runny.

2 In a large pan, dissolve the salt in the distilled or previously boiled water. Add the peppercorns, then allow the water to cool and add the spirit.

3 Gently tap the eggs all over but do NOT peel them. Place in a large, airtight, sterilized jar and fill up with the liquid, totally covering the eggs. Seal the jar and leave the eggs to stand in a cool, dark place for 7–8 days.

4 To serve, remove the eggs from the liquid and peel off the shells carefully. Cut each egg in half or quarters and serve whole with a dipping sauce and a bowl of toasted sesame seeds.

> ## COOK'S TIP
>
> • Although you can buy Chinese dipping sauces in the supermarket, it is very easy to make your own at home. To make a quick dipping sauce, mix equal quantities of soy sauce and hoisin sauce.
> • Be sure to use only boiled water or distilled water for the eggs, as the water must be completely free of bacteria or it will enter the porous shells.

Eggs Mimosa

Mimosa describes the fine yellow and white grated egg which looks not unlike the flower of the same name. It can be used to finish any dish, adding a light summery touch.

INGREDIENTS

Serves 20

12 hard-boiled (hard-cooked) eggs, peeled
2 ripe avocados, halved and
    stoned (pitted)
1 garlic clove, crushed
Tabasco sauce, to taste
15ml/1 tbsp virgin olive oil
salt and ground black pepper
20 chicory (Belgian endive) leaves or
    small crisp green lettuce leaves, to serve
basil leaves, to garnish

1 Reserve 2 eggs, halve the remainder and put the yolks in a mixing bowl. Blend or beat the yolks with the avocados, garlic, Tabasco sauce, oil and salt and pepper. Check the seasoning. Pipe or spoon this mixture back into the halved egg whites.

2 Sieve the remaining egg whites and sprinkle over the filled eggs. Sieve the yolks on top. Arrange each half egg on a chicory or lettuce leaf and place them on a serving platter. Sprinkle the basil leaves over the filled egg halves before serving.

Roquefort and Pear Sandwich

Pears seem to have a natural affinity for blue cheese, and the rocket adds a delicious peppery note.

Makes 4

3 slices brioche loaf

115g/4oz/½ cup cream cheese

few sprigs rocket (arugula)

115g/4oz Roquefort cheese, sliced

1 ripe pear

juice of ½ lemon

4 pecan nuts, to garnish

viola flowers, to garnish
   (optional)

1 Toast the brioche and spread with cream cheese.

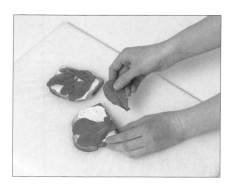

2 Arrange the rocket leaves on top of the cream cheese.

3 Place the sliced Roquefort cheese on top of the rocket.

4 Quarter, core and slice the pear then brush with lemon juice to prevent discoloration.

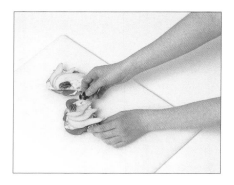

5 Arrange the pear slices, overlapping in a fan shape on the Roquefort cheese.

6 Garnish with pecan nuts (whole or chopped) and a viola flower if you wish.

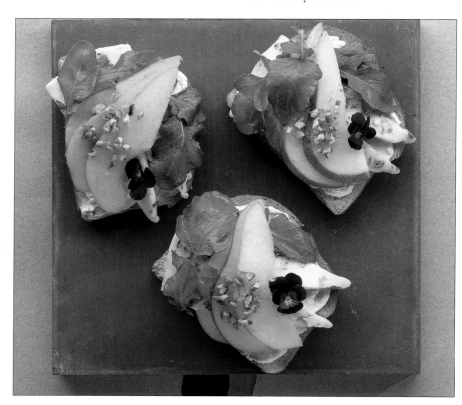

COOK'S TIP

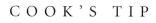

Other blue cheeses, such as Gorgonzola, will also work well in this dish.

Prawn and Vegetable Crostini

Use bottled carciofini (tiny artichoke hearts preserved in olive oil) for this simple first course, which can be prepared very quickly.

INGREDIENTS

Serves 4

450g/1lb unpeeled cooked prawns (shrimp)

4 slices of ciabatta, cut diagonally across

3 garlic cloves, peeled and 2 halved lengthwise

60ml/4 tbsp olive oil

200g/7oz/2 cups small button (white) mushrooms, trimmed

12 drained bottled carciofini

60ml/4 tbsp chopped flat leaf parsley

salt and ground black pepper

1 Peel the prawns and remove the heads. Rub the ciabatta slices on both sides with the cut sides of the halved garlic cloves, drizzle with a little olive oil and grill (broil) until lightly browned.

2 Finely chop the remaining garlic. Heat the remaining oil in a frying pan and gently fry the chopped garlic until golden, but do not allow it to burn.

3 Add the mushrooms and stir to coat with oil. Season and sauté for about 2–3 minutes. Gently stir in the drained carciofini, then add the chopped flat leaf parsley.

4 Season again, then stir in the prawns and sauté briefly to warm through. Pile the prawn mixture on to the ciabatta. Pour over any remaining cooking juices and serve immediately.

COOK'S TIP

Don't be tempted to use thawed frozen prawns, especially those that have been peeled. Freshly cooked prawns in their shells are infinitely nicer.

Smoked Salmon and Gravlax Sauce

Gravlax is cured fresh salmon: it is marinated in dill, salt and sugar and left for 2–3 days with weights on it. It can now be bought in most supermarkets and delicatessens and you can use it instead of smoked salmon if you wish.

3 Add a little frisée lettuce and a slice each of lemon and cucumber. Spoon over some Gravlax sauce, then garnish with dill.

INGREDIENTS

Serves 8

25g/1oz/2 tbsp softened butter

5ml/1 tsp grated lemon rind

4 slices rye or pumpernickel bread

115g/4oz smoked salmon

few leaves frisée lettuce

8 lemon slices

8 cucumber slices

60ml/4 tbsp Gravlax sauce

dill sprigs, to garnish

1 Mix the butter and lemon rind together, spread over the bread and cut in half diagonally.

2 Arrange the smoked salmon over the top to cover.

King Prawns in Crispy Batter

The Asian-style dipping sauce is a perfect accompaniment to these irresistible crispy snacks.

INGREDIENTS

Serves 4

120ml/4fl oz/½ cup water

1 egg

115g/4oz/1 cup plain (all-purpose) flour

5ml/1 tsp cayenne pepper

12 raw king prawns (jumbo shrimp), unpeeled

vegetable oil, for deep-frying

flat leaf parsley, to garnish

lemon wedges, to serve

For the dipping sauce

30ml/2 tbsp soy sauce

30ml/2 tbsp dry sherry

10ml/2 tsp clear honey

3 To make the dipping sauce, stir together the soy sauce, dry sherry and honey in a small bowl until well combined.

4 Heat the oil in a large pan or deep-fryer, until a cube of stale bread tossed in browns in 1 minute.

5 Holding the prawns by their tails, dip them into the batter, one at a time, shaking off any excess. Drop the prawns carefully into the oil and fry for 2–3 minutes until crisp and golden brown. Drain on kitchen paper and serve with the dipping sauce and lemon wedges, garnished with parsley.

1 In a large bowl, whisk the water with the egg. Add the flour and cayenne, and whisk until smooth.

2 Carefully peel the prawns, leaving just the tail sections intact. Make a shallow cut down the back of each prawn, then pull out and discard the dark intestinal tract.

COOK'S TIP

Use leftover batter to coat thin strips of sweet potato, beetroot (beets), carrot or (bell) pepper, then deep-fry until golden.

Tapenade and Quail's Eggs

Tapenade is a purée made from capers, olives and anchovies. It is popularly used in Mediterranean cooking. It complements the taste of eggs perfectly, especially quail's eggs, which look very pretty on open sandwiches.

INGREDIENTS

Serves 8

8 quail's eggs

1 small baguette

45ml/3 tbsp tapenade

frisée lettuce leaves

3 small tomatoes, sliced

2–4 pitted black olives

4 canned anchovy fillets, drained and
   halved lengthways

parsley sprigs, to garnish

1 Boil the quail's eggs for 4 minutes, then plunge them straight into cold water to cool. Crack the shells and remove them very carefully.

2 Cut the baguette into slices on the diagonal and spread each one with some of the tapenade.

3 Arrange a little frisée lettuce, torn to fit, and the tomato slices on top.

4 Halve the quail's eggs and place them on top of the tomato slices.

5 Finish with a little more tapenade, the olives and finally the anchovies. Garnish with small parsley sprigs.

COOK'S TIP

To make 300ml/½ pint/1¼ cups of tuna tapenade, put 90g/3½oz canned drained tuna in a food processor with 25g/1oz/2 tbsp capers, 10 canned anchovy fillets and 75g/3oz/¾ cup pitted black olives and blend until smooth, scraping down the sides as necessary. Gradually add 60ml/ 4 tbsp olive oil through the feeder tube. This purée can be used for filling hard-boiled (hard-cooked) eggs. Blend the tapenade with the egg yolks then pile into the whites.

Potato Blinis

These light pancakes originate from Russia, where they are served with caviar.

INGREDIENTS

Serves 6

115g/4oz maincrop potatoes, boiled
   and mashed

15ml/1 tbsp easy-blend (rapid-rise)
   dried yeast

175g/6oz/1½ cups plain (all-purpose)
   flour

oil, for greasing

90ml/6 tbsp sour cream

6 slices smoked salmon

salt and ground black pepper

lemon slices, to garnish

1 In a large bowl, mix together the potatoes, dried yeast, flour and 300ml/½ pint/1¼ cups lukewarm water.

2 Leave to rise in a warm place for about 30 minutes until the mixture has doubled in size.

3 Heat a non-stick frying pan and add a little oil. Drop spoonfuls of the mixture on to the preheated pan. Cook the blinis for 2 minutes until lightly golden on the underside, toss with a spatula and cook on the second side for about 1 minute.

4 Season the blinis with some salt and pepper. Serve with a little sour cream and a small slice of smoked salmon folded on top. Garnish with a final grind of black pepper and a small slice of lemon.

COOK'S TIP

These small pancakes can easily be prepared in advance. Simply reheat them in a low oven.

Tuna in Rolled Red Peppers

This lovely savoury combination originated in southern Italy. The peppers have a sweet, smoky taste that combines particularly well with a robust fish like tuna. You could try canned mackerel instead.

INGREDIENTS

Serves 8–10

3 large red (bell) peppers

200g/7oz can tuna, drained

30ml/2 tbsp lemon juice

45ml/3 tbsp olive oil

6 green or black olives, pitted
    and chopped

30ml/2 tbsp chopped fresh parsley

1 garlic clove, finely chopped

1 celery stick, very finely chopped

salt and ground black pepper

1 Place the peppers under a hot grill (broiler), and turn occasionally until they are black and blistered on all sides. Remove from the heat and place in a plastic bag.

2 Leave for 5 minutes, and then peel. Cut the peppers into quarters, and remove the stems, seeds and pith.

3 Meanwhile, flake the tuna and combine with the lemon juice and oil. Stir in the olives, parsley, garlic and celery. Season with salt and plenty of ground black pepper.

4 Lay the pepper segments out flat, skin-side down. Divide the tuna mixture equally among them. Spread it out, pressing it into an even layer. Roll the peppers up. Place the pepper rolls in the refrigerator for at least 1 hour. Just before serving, cut each roll in half with a sharp knife.

Ham and Asparagus Slice

Be creative in your arrangement of the ingredients here. You could make ham cornets, or wrap the asparagus in the ham, or use different meats, such as salami, mortadella or Black Forest ham.

INGREDIENTS

Serves 4

12 asparagus spears
115g/4oz/½ cup cream cheese
4 slices rye bread
4 slices ham
few leaves frisée lettuce
30ml/2 tbsp mayonnaise
4 radish roses, to garnish

1 Cook the asparagus until tender, drain, pat dry with kitchen paper and cool.

2 Spread cream cheese over the rye bread and arrange the ham in folds over the top.

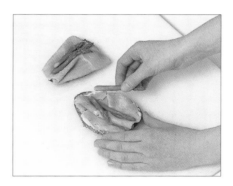

3 Lay 3 asparagus spears on each sandwich.

4 Arrange frisée lettuce on the sandwiches and spoon over some mayonnaise.

5 Garnish with radish roses. Serve extra mayonnaise separately if you like.

Eggy Thai Fish Cakes

These tangy little fish cakes, with a kick of Eastern spice, make great party food, or made slightly larger, can be a great appetizer too.

INGREDIENTS

Makes about 20

225g/8oz smoked cod or haddock
225g/8oz fresh cod or haddock
1 small fresh red chilli, seeded and
  finely chopped
2 garlic cloves, grated
1 lemon grass stalk, very finely chopped
2 large spring onions (scallions), very
  finely chopped
30ml/2 tbsp Thai fish sauce (nam pla) or
  30ml/2 tbsp soy sauce and a few drops
  anchovy essence
60ml/4 tbsp thick coconut milk
2 large (US extra large) eggs,
  lightly beaten
15ml/1 tbsp chopped coriander (cilantro)
15ml/1 tbsp cornflour (cornstarch), plus
  extra for moulding
oil, for frying
soy sauce, rice vinegar or Thai fish sauce
  (nam pla), for dipping

1 Place the prepared smoked fish in a bowl of cold water and leave to soak for 10 minutes. Dry well on kitchen paper. Chop the smoked and fresh fish roughly and place in a food processor.

2 Add the chilli, garlic, lemon grass, onions, the sauce and the coconut milk. Process until the fish is well blended with the spices, then add the eggs and coriander and process for a further few seconds. Cover with clear film (plastic wrap) and chill for 1 hour.

3 To make the fish cakes, flour your hands with cornflour and shape large teaspoonfuls into neat balls, coating them with the flour.

4 Heat 5–7.5cm/2–3in oil in a medium pan until a crust of bread turns golden in about 1 minute. Fry the fish balls 5–6 at a time, turning them carefully with a slotted spoon for 2–3 minutes, until they turn golden all over. Remove with a slotted spoon and drain on kitchen paper. Keep the fish cakes warm in the oven until they are all cooked. Serve immediately with one or more dipping sauces.

Dates Stuffed with Chorizo

This is a delicious combination from Spain, using fresh dates and spicy chorizo sausage.

INGREDIENTS

Serves 4–6

50g/2oz chorizo

12 fresh dates, pitted

6 streaky (fatty) bacon rashers (strips)

oil, for frying

plain (all-purpose) flour, for dusting

1 egg, beaten

50g/2oz/1 cup fresh breadcrumbs

1 Trim the ends of the chorizo and then peel away the skin. Cut into 3 x 2cm/³⁄₄ in slices. Cut these in half lengthways, then into quarters, giving 12 pieces.

2 Stuff each date with a piece of chorizo, closing the date around it. Stretch the bacon, by running the back of a knife along the rasher. Cut each rasher in half, widthwise. Wrap a piece of bacon around each date and secure with a wooden cocktail stick (toothpick).

3 In a deep pan, heat 1cm/½ in of oil. Dust the dates with flour, dip them in the beaten egg, then coat in breadcrumbs. Fry the dates in the hot oil, turning them, until golden. Remove the dates with a slotted spoon, and drain on kitchen paper. Serve.

Chicken Liver Pâté

This rich-tasting, smooth pâté will keep in the refrigerator for about 3 days. Serve with thick slices of hot toast or warm bread – a rustic olive oil bread such as ciabatta would be ideal.

INGREDIENTS

Serves 8

115g/4oz chicken livers, thawed if
    frozen, trimmed

1 small garlic clove, chopped

5ml/1 tbsp sherry

30ml/2 tbsp brandy

50g/2oz/¼ cup butter, melted

¼ teaspoon salt

fresh herbs and black peppercorns,
    to garnish

hot toast or warm bread, to serve

1 Preheat the oven to 150°/300°F/Gas 2. Place the chicken livers and chopped garlic in a food processor or blender and process until smooth.

2 With the motor running, gradually add the sherry, brandy, melted butter and salt.

3 Pour the mixture into 2 x 7.5cm/3in ramekins and cover with foil.

4 Place the ramekins in a small roasting pan and pour in boiling water until it comes halfway up the sides of the ramekins.

5 Carefully transfer the pan to the oven and bake for 20 minutes. Let cool to room temperature, then remove the ramekins from the pan and chill until ready to serve. Serve the pâté with hot toast or warm bread, garnished with fresh herbs and black peppercorns.

Chorizo Pastry Puffs

These flaky pastry puffs, filled with spicy chorizo sausage and grated cheese, make a really superb accompaniment to a glass of cold sherry or beer. You can use any type of hard cheese for the puffs, but for best results, choose a mild variety, as the chorizo has plenty of flavour.

INGREDIENTS

Serves 8

225g/8oz puff pastry, thawed if frozen

115g/4oz cured chorizo,
   finely chopped

50g/2oz/½ cup grated cheese

1 small egg (US medium), beaten

5ml/1 tsp paprika

1 Roll out the pastry thinly on a floured work surface. Using a 7.5cm/3in cutter, stamp out as many rounds as possible, then re-roll the trimmings, if necessary, and stamp out more rounds to make 16 in all.

2 Preheat the oven to 230°C/450°F/Gas 8. Put the chopped chorizo and grated cheese in a bowl and toss together lightly.

3 Lay one of the pastry rounds in the palm of your hand and place a little of the chorizo mixture across the centre.

4 Using your other hand, pinch the edges of the pastry together along the top to seal, as when making a miniature patty. Repeat the process with the remaining rounds to make 16 puffs in all.

5 Place the pastries on a non-stick baking sheet and brush lightly with the beaten egg. Using a small sifter or tea strainer, dust the tops lightly with a little of the paprika.

6 Bake the pastries in the oven for 10–12 minutes, until puffed and golden brown. Transfer the pastries to a wire rack. Leave to cool for 5 minutes, then serve the chorizo pastry puffs warm, dusted with the remaining paprika.

Mini Sausage Rolls

These miniature versions of old-fashioned sausage rolls are always popular – the Parmesan cheese gives them an extra special flavour.

Makes about 48

15g/½ oz/1 tbsp butter

1 onion, finely chopped

350g/12oz good-quality sausage meat
    (bulk sausage)

15ml/1 tbsp dried mixed herbs such as
    oregano, thyme, sage, tarragon or dill

25g/1oz finely chopped pistachio nuts

350g/12oz puff pastry, thawed if frozen

60–90ml/4–6 tbsp freshly grated
    Parmesan cheese

salt and ground black pepper

1 egg, lightly beaten, for glazing

poppy seeds, sesame seeds, fennel seeds
    and aniseed (anise seed), for sprinkling

1 In a small frying pan, over a medium heat, melt the butter. Add the onion and cook for about 5 minutes, until softened. Remove from the heat and cool. Put the onion, sausage meat, herbs, salt and pepper and nuts in a mixing bowl and stir together until completely blended.

2 Divide the sausage mixture into 4 equal portions and roll into thin sausages measuring about 25cm/10in long. Set aside.

3 On a lightly floured surface, roll out the pastry to about 3mm/⅛in thick. Cut the pastry into 4 strips 25 x 7.5cm/10 x 3in. Place a long sausage on each pastry strip and sprinkle each with a little Parmesan cheese.

COOK'S TIP

Filo pastry can be used instead of puff pastry for a very light effect. Depending on the size of the filo sheets, cut into 8 pieces 25 x 7.5cm/10 x 3in. Brush 4 of the sheets with a little melted butter or vegetable oil and place a second pastry sheet on top. Place 1 sausage log on each of the 4 layered sheets and roll up and bake as above.

4 Brush 1 long edge of each of the pastry strips with the egg glaze and roll up to enclose each sausage. Set them seam-side down and press gently to seal. Brush each with the egg glaze and sprinkle with one type of seeds. Repeat with remaining pastry strips, using different seeds.

5 Preheat the oven to 220°C/425°F/Gas 7. Lightly grease a large baking sheet. Cut each of the pastry logs into 2.5cm/1in lengths and arrange on the baking sheet. Bake for about 15 minutes until the pastry is crisp and brown. Serve warm or allow to cool before serving.

Fork Food

These lovely, tasty morsels, which are often served hot or with sauces, require just a fork to eat neatly. Delicious dishes such as Sesame Seed-coated Falafal with Tahini Dip and Risotto Frittata represent flavours from around the world and would make a bountiful buffet supper.

Spicy Peanut Balls

Tasty rice balls, rolled in chopped peanuts and deep-fried, make a delicious first course. Serve them as they are, or with a chilli sauce for dipping. Make sure there are plenty of napkins to hand.

INGREDIENTS

Makes 16

1 garlic clove, crushed

1cm/½ in piece fresh root ginger, peeled and finely chopped

1.5ml/¼ tsp turmeric

5ml/1 tsp granulated sugar

2.5ml/½ tsp salt

5ml/1 tsp chilli sauce

10ml/2 tsp fish sauce or soy sauce

30ml/2 tbsp chopped coriander (cilantro)

juice of ½ lime

225g/8oz/2 cups cooked white long grain rice

115g/4oz/1 cup peanuts, chopped

vegetable oil, for deep-frying

lime wedges and chilli dipping sauce, to serve (optional)

1 Process the garlic, ginger and turmeric in a food processor or blender until the mixture forms a paste. Add the sugar, salt, chilli sauce and fish sauce or soy sauce, with the chopped coriander and lime juice. Process briefly to mix the ingredients.

2 Add three-quarters of the cooked rice to the paste in the food processor and process until smooth and sticky. Scrape into a mixing bowl and stir in the remainder of the rice. Wet your hands and shape the mixture into thumb-size balls.

3 Roll the balls in the chopped peanuts, making sure they are evenly coated.

4 Heat the oil in a deep-fryer or wok. Deep-fry the peanut balls until crisp. Drain on kitchen paper and then pile on to a platter. Serve hot with lime wedges and a chilli dipping sauce, if using.

Dolmades

If you can't locate fresh vine leaves, use a packet or can of brined leaves. Like fresh vine leaves these too must be soaked in hot water before use.

INGREDIENTS

Makes 20 to 24

24–28 fresh young vine (grape)
  leaves, soaked
30ml/2 tbsp olive oil
1 large onion, finely chopped
1 garlic clove, crushed
225g/8oz/2 cups cooked long grain rice, or
  mixed white and wild rice
about 45ml/3 tbsp pine nuts
15ml/1 tbsp flaked (sliced) almonds
40g/1½ oz/¼ cup sultanas
  (golden raisins)
15ml/1 tbsp chopped fresh chives
15ml/1 tbsp finely chopped fresh mint
juice of ½ lemon
150ml/¼ pint/⅔ cup white wine
hot vegetable stock
salt and ground black pepper
mint sprig, to garnish
garlic yogurt and pitta bread, to serve

1 Bring a large pan of water to the boil and cook the vine leaves for about 2–3 minutes. They will darken and go limp after about 1 minute and simmering for a further minute or so will ensure they are pliable. If using packet or canned leaves, place in a bowl, cover with boiling water and leave for 20 minutes until the leaves can be separated easily. Rinse and dry on kitchen paper.

2 Heat the oil in a small frying pan and fry the onion and garlic for 3–4 minutes over a gentle heat until soft. Spoon the mixture into a large bowl and add the cooked rice. Stir to combine.

3 Stir in 30ml/2 tbsp of the pine nuts, the almonds, sultanas, chives and mint. Squeeze in the lemon juice. Add salt and pepper to taste and mix well.

4 Set aside 4 large vine leaves. Lay a vine leaf on a clean work surface, veined side uppermost. Place a spoonful of filling near the stem, fold the lower part of the vine leaf over it and roll up, folding in the sides as you go. Stuff the rest of the vine leaves in the same way.

5 Line the base of a deep frying pan with the reserved vine leaves. Place the dolmades close together in the pan, seam side down, in a single layer. Pour over the wine and enough stock to just cover. Anchor the dolmades by placing a plate on top of them, then cover the pan and simmer gently for 30 minutes.

6 Transfer the dolmades to a plate. Cool, chill, then garnish with the remaining pine nuts and the mint. Serve with a little garlic yogurt and some pitta bread.

Thai Tempeh Cakes with Dipping Sauce

Made from soya beans, tempeh is similar to tofu or beancurd but has a nuttier taste. Here, it is combined with a fragrant blend of lemon grass, coriander and ginger, and formed into small patties.

INGREDIENTS

Makes 8 cakes

1 lemon grass stalk, outer leaves removed, finely chopped

2 garlic cloves, finely chopped

2 spring onions (scallions), finely chopped

2 shallots, finely chopped

2 chillies, seeded and finely chopped

2.5cm/1 in piece fresh root ginger, finely chopped

60ml/4 tbsp chopped coriander (cilantro), plus extra to garnish

250g/9oz/2¼ cups tempeh, defrosted if frozen, sliced

15ml/1 tbsp lime juice

5ml/1 tsp caster (superfine) sugar

45ml/3 tbsp plain (all-purpose) flour

1 large (US extra large) egg, lightly beaten

vegetable oil, for frying

salt and ground black pepper

For the dipping sauce

45ml/3 tbsp mirin

45ml/3 tbsp white wine vinegar

2 spring onions (scallions), finely sliced

15ml/1 tbsp sugar

2 chillies, finely chopped

30ml/2 tbsp chopped coriander (cilantro)

large pinch of salt

1 To make the dipping sauce, mix together the mirin, vinegar, spring onions, sugar, chillies, coriander and salt in a small bowl and set aside.

2 Place the lemon grass, garlic, spring onions, shallots, chillies, ginger and coriander in a food processor or blender, then process to a coarse paste. Add the tempeh, lime juice and sugar, then blend until combined. Add the flour and egg, and season well. Process again until the mixture forms a coarse, sticky paste.

3 Take a heaped tablespoon of the tempeh paste mixture at a time and form into rounds with your hands. The mixture will be quite sticky.

4 Heat enough oil to cover the base of a large frying pan. Fry the tempeh cakes for 5–6 minutes, turning once, until golden. Drain on kitchen paper and serve warm with the dipping sauce, garnished with chopped fresh coriander.

Sesame Seed-coated Falafel with Tahini Dip

Sesame seeds are used to give a delightfully crunchy coating to these spicy chickpea patties. Serve with the tahini yogurt dip.

INGREDIENTS

Serves 6

250g/9oz/1⅓ cups dried chickpeas

2 garlic cloves, crushed

1 red chilli, seeded and finely sliced

5ml/1 tsp ground coriander

5ml/1 tsp ground cumin

15ml/1 tbsp chopped fresh mint

15ml/1 tbsp chopped fresh parsley

2 spring onions (scallions), finely chopped

1 large (US extra large) egg, beaten

sesame seeds, for coating

sunflower oil, for frying

salt and ground black pepper

For the tahini yogurt dip

30ml/2 tbsp light tahini

200g/7oz/scant 1 cup natural (plain)
   live yogurt

5ml/1 tsp cayenne pepper, plus extra
   for sprinkling

15ml/1 tbsp chopped fresh mint

1 spring onion (scallion), finely sliced

fresh herbs, to garnish

1 Place the chickpeas in a bowl, cover with cold water and leave to soak overnight. Drain and rinse the chickpeas, then place in a pan and cover with cold water. Bring to the boil and boil rapidly for 10 minutes. Reduce the heat; simmer for about 1 hour until tender.

2 Meanwhile, make the tahini yogurt dip. Mix together the tahini, yogurt, cayenne pepper and mint in a small bowl. Sprinkle the spring onion and extra cayenne pepper on top and chill in the refrigerator until required.

3 Combine the chickpeas with the garlic, chilli, ground spices, herbs, spring onions and seasoning, then mix in the egg. Place in a food processor and blend until the mixture forms a coarse paste. If the paste seems too soft, chill it for 30 minutes.

4 Form the chilled chickpea paste into 12 patties with your hands, then roll each one in the sesame seeds to coat thoroughly.

5 Heat enough oil to cover the base of a large frying pan. Fry the falafel, in batches if necessary, for 6 minutes, turning once. Serve with the tahini yogurt dip, garnished with fresh herbs.

Baked Mediterranean Vegetables

Crisp and golden crunchy batter surrounds these vegetables, turning them into a substantial first course or a lighter main course. Use other vegetables instead if you prefer.

INGREDIENTS

Serves 10–12

1 small aubergine (eggplant), trimmed, halved and thickly sliced

1 egg

115g/4oz/1 cup plain (all-purpose) flour

300ml/½ pint/1¼ cups milk

30ml/2 tbsp fresh thyme leaves, or 10ml/2 tsp dried

1 red onion

2 large courgettes (zucchini)

1 red (bell) pepper

1 yellow (bell) pepper

60–75ml/4–5 tbsp sunflower oil

salt and ground black pepper

30ml/2 tbsp freshly grated Parmesan cheese and fresh herbs, to garnish

1 Place the aubergine in a colander or sieve, sprinkle generously with salt and leave for 10 minutes. Drain and pat dry on kitchen paper.

2 Meanwhile, to make the batter, beat the egg, then gradually beat in the flour and a little milk to make a smooth thick paste. Blend in the rest of the milk, add the thyme leaves and seasoning to taste and blend until smooth. Leave in a cool place until required.

3 Quarter the onion and slice the courgettes and seed and quarter the peppers. Put the oil in a roasting pan and heat through in the oven at 220°C/425°F/Gas 7. Add all the vegetables, turn in the fat to coat them well and return to the oven for 20 minutes until they start to cook.

4 Give the batter another whisk then pour over the vegetables and return to the oven for 30 minutes. If well puffed up and golden, then reduce the heat to 190°C/375°F/Gas 5 for another 10–15 minutes until crisp around the edges. Sprinkle with Parmesan and herbs and serve.

COOK'S TIP

It is essential to get the fat in the dish really hot before adding the batter, or it will not rise well. Use a dish which is not too deep.

Risotto Frittata

*Half omelette, half risotto, this
makes a delightful and satisfying
dish. If possible, cook each frittata
separately, and preferably in a
small, cast-iron pan, so that the eggs
cook quickly underneath but stay
moist on top. Or cook in one large
pan and serve in wedges.*

INGREDIENTS

Serves 4

30–45ml/2–3 tbsp olive oil

1 small onion, finely chopped

1 garlic clove, crushed

1 large red (bell) pepper, seeded and cut
   into thin strips

150g/5oz/¾ cup risotto rice

400–475ml/14–16fl oz/1⅔–2 cups
   simmering vegetable stock

25–40g/1–1½ oz/2–3 tbsp butter

175g/6oz/2½ cups button (white)
   mushrooms, finely sliced

60ml/4 tbsp freshly grated
   Parmesan cheese

6–8 eggs

salt and ground black pepper

1 Heat 15ml/1 tbsp oil in a large
frying pan and fry the onion
and garlic over a gentle heat for
2–3 minutes until the onion begins
to soften but does not brown. Add
the pepper and cook, stirring, for
4–5 minutes, until soft.

2 Stir in the rice and cook gently
for 2–3 minutes, stirring all the
time, until the grains are evenly
coated with oil.

3 Add one-quarter of the
vegetable stock and season
with salt and pepper. Stir over a
low heat until the stock has been
absorbed. Continue to add more
stock, a little at a time, allowing the
rice to absorb the liquid before
adding more. Continue cooking in
this way until the rice is *al dente*.

4 In a separate small pan, heat a
little of the remaining oil and
some of the butter and quickly fry
the mushrooms until golden.
Transfer to a plate.

5 When the rice is tender,
remove from the heat and stir
in the cooked mushrooms and the
Parmesan cheese.

6 Beat together the eggs with
40ml/8 tsp cold water and
season well. Heat the remaining oil
and butter in an omelette pan and
add the risotto mixture. Spread the
mixture out in the pan, then
immediately add the beaten egg,
tilting the pan so that the omelette
cooks evenly. Fry over a moderately
high heat for 1–2 minutes, then
transfer to a warmed plate and serve.

COOK'S TIP

Don't be impatient while cooking
the rice. Adding the stock
gradually ensures a wonderfully
creamy consistency.

Deep-fried New Potatoes with Saffron Aioli

Serve these crispy little golden potatoes dipped into a wickedly garlic-flavoured mayonnaise – then sit back and watch them disappear in a matter of minutes!

INGREDIENTS

Serves 4

1 egg yolk

2.5ml/½ tsp Dijon mustard

300ml/½ pint/1¼ cups extra virgin olive oil

15–30ml/1–2 tbsp lemon juice

1 garlic clove, crushed

2.5ml/½ tsp saffron threads

20 baby, new or salad potatoes

vegetable oil, for deep-frying

salt and ground black pepper

1 For the saffron aioli, put the egg yolk in a bowl with the Dijon mustard and a pinch of salt. Stir to mix together well. Beat in the olive oil very slowly, drop by drop at first and then in a very thin stream. Stir in the lemon juice.

2 Season the aioli with salt and pepper then add the crushed garlic and beat into the mixture thoroughly to combine.

3 Place the saffron in a small bowl and add 10ml/2 tsp hot water. Press the saffron with the back of a teaspoon, to extract the colour and flavour, and leave to infuse for 5 minutes. Beat the saffron and the liquid into the aioli.

4 Cook the potatoes in their skins in boiling salted water for 5 minutes, then turn off the heat. Cover the pan and leave for 15 minutes. Drain the potatoes, then dry them thoroughly in a dishtowel.

5 Heat a 1cm/½in layer of vegetable oil in a deep pan. When the oil is very hot, add the potatoes and fry quickly, turning them constantly, until crisp and golden all over. Drain on kitchen paper and serve hot with the saffron aioli.

Chilli Cheese Tortilla with Tomato Salsa

Good warm or cold, this is like a quiche without the pastry base. Cheese and chillies are more than a match for each other.

Serves 8

45ml/3 tbsp sunflower or olive oil

1 small onion, thinly sliced

2–3 green jalapeño chillies, sliced

200g/7oz cold cooked potato, thinly sliced

120g/4¼ oz/generous 1 cup grated
   Manchego, Mexican queso blanco or
   Monterey Jack cheese

6 eggs, beaten

salt and ground black pepper

fresh herbs, to garnish

For the salsa

500g/1¼ lb fresh flavoursome tomatoes,
   peeled, seeded and finely chopped

1 green chilli, seeded and finely chopped

2 garlic cloves, crushed

45ml/3 tbsp chopped coriander (cilantro)

juice of 1 lime

2.5ml/½ tsp salt

1 Make the salsa. Put the tomatoes in a bowl with the rest of the ingredients. Mix well and set aside.

2 Heat half the oil in a large omelette pan and gently fry the onion and jalapeños for 5 minutes, stirring once or twice, until softened. Add the potato and cook for a further 5 minutes until lightly browned, taking care to keep the slices whole.

3 Using a slotted spoon, transfer the vegetables to a warm plate. Wipe the pan with kitchen paper, then pour in the remaining oil. Heat well and return the vegetable mixture to the pan. Sprinkle the cheese over the top.

4 Pour in the beaten egg, making sure that it seeps under the vegetables. Cook the tortilla over a gentle heat until set. Serve in wedges, garnished with fresh herbs, with the salsa on the side.

COOK'S TIP

If you cannot find the cheeses listed, use a medium Cheddar cheese instead.

Lemon, Thyme and Bean Stuffed Mushrooms

Portabello mushrooms have a rich flavour and a meaty texture that go well with this fragrant herb-and-lemon stuffing. The garlic-flavoured pine nut accompaniment is a traditional Middle Eastern dish with a smooth, creamy consistency similar to that of hummus.

INGREDIENTS

Serves 4–6

200g/7oz/1 cup dried or 400g/14oz/2 cups
   drained, canned aduki beans
45ml/3 tbsp olive oil, plus extra
   for brushing
1 onion, finely chopped
2 garlic cloves, crushed
30ml/2 tbsp fresh chopped thyme or
   5ml/1 tsp dried
8 large field mushrooms, such as
   portabello mushrooms, stalks
   finely chopped
50g/2oz/1 cup fresh wholemeal (whole-
   wheat) breadcrumbs
juice of 1 lemon
185g/6½ oz/¾ cup goat's cheese,
   crumbled
salt and ground black pepper

For the pine nut sauce
50g/2oz/½ cup pine nuts, toasted
50g/2oz/1 cup cubed white bread
2 garlic cloves, chopped
200ml/7fl oz/scant 1 cup milk
45ml/3 tbsp olive oil
15ml/1 tbsp chopped fresh parsley, to
   garnish (optional)

1 If using dried beans, soak them overnight, then drain and rinse well. Place in a pan, add enough water to cover and bring to the boil. Boil rapidly for 10 minutes, then reduce the heat, cook for 30 minutes until tender, then drain. If using canned beans, rinse, drain well, then set aside.

2 Preheat the oven to 200°C/ 400°F/Gas 6. Heat the oil in a large heavy pan, add the onion and garlic and sauté for 5 minutes until softened. Add the thyme and the mushroom stalks and cook for a further 3 minutes, stirring occasionally, until tender.

3 Stir in the beans, breadcrumbs and lemon juice, season well, then cook for 2 minutes until heated through. Mash two-thirds of the beans with a fork or potato masher, leaving the remaining beans whole.

4 Brush a baking dish and the base and sides of the mushrooms with oil, then top each one with a spoonful of the bean mixture. Place the mushrooms in the dish, cover with foil and bake for 20 minutes. Remove the foil. Top each mushroom with some of the goat's cheese and bake for a further 15 minutes, or until the cheese is melted and bubbly and the mushrooms are tender.

5 To make the pine nut sauce, place all the ingredients in a food processor or blender and blend until smooth and creamy. Add more milk if the mixture appears too thick. Sprinkle with parsley, if using, and serve with the stuffed mushrooms.

Grilled King Prawns with Romesco Sauce

This sauce, originally from the Catalan region of Spain, is served with fish and shellfish. Its main ingredients are sweet pepper, tomatoes, garlic and almonds.

Serves 6–8

24 raw king prawns (large shrimp)
30–45ml/2–3 tbsp olive oil
flat leaf parsley, to garnish
lemon wedges, to serve

For the sauce
2 well-flavoured tomatoes
60ml/4 tbsp olive oil
1 onion, chopped
4 garlic cloves, chopped
1 canned pimiento, chopped
2.5ml/½ tsp dried chilli flakes or powder
75ml/5 tbsp fish stock
30ml/2 tbsp white wine
10 blanched almonds
15ml/1 tbsp red wine vinegar
salt, to taste

3 Toast the almonds under the grill (broiler) until golden. Transfer to a blender or food processor and grind coarsely. Add the remaining 30ml/2 tbsp of olive oil, the vinegar and the last garlic clove and process until evenly combined. Add the tomato and pimiento sauce and process until smooth. Season with salt, to taste.

4 Remove the heads from the prawns leaving them otherwise unpeeled and, with a sharp knife, slit each one down the back and remove the dark vein. Rinse and pat dry on kitchen paper. Preheat the grill. Toss the prawns in olive oil, then spread out in the grill (broiling) pan. Grill (broil) for about 2–3 minutes on each side, until pink. Arrange on a serving platter with the lemon wedges, and the sauce in a small bowl. Serve garnished with parsley.

1 To make the sauce, immerse the tomatoes in boiling water for about 30 seconds, then refresh them under cold water. Peel away the skins and roughly chop the tomato flesh.

2 Heat 30ml/2 tbsp of the oil in a pan, add the onion and 3 of the garlic cloves and cook until soft. Add the pimiento, tomatoes, chilli, fish stock and wine, then cover and simmer for 30 minutes.

Fish Sausages

This recipe originated in Hungary during the seventeenth century. It is still popular today.

INGREDIENTS

Serves 4

375g/13oz fish fillets, such as perch, pike, carp or cod, skinned

1 white bread roll

75ml/5 tbsp milk

25ml/1½ tbsp chopped fresh flat leaf parsley

2 eggs, well beaten

50g/2oz/½ cup plain (all-purpose) flour

50g/2oz/1 cup fine fresh white breadcrumbs

oil, for shallow frying

salt and ground black pepper

deep-fried parsley sprigs and lemon wedges, dusted with paprika, to garnish

1 Mince (grind) or process the fish coarsely in a food processor or blender. Soak the roll in the milk for about 10 minutes, then squeeze it out. Mix the fish and bread together before adding the chopped parsley, one of the eggs and plenty of seasoning.

2 Using your fingers, shape the fish mixture into 10cm/4in long sausages, making them about 2.5cm/1 in thick.

3 Carefully roll the fish sausages in the flour, then in the remaining egg and finally in the breadcrumbs.

4 Heat the oil in a pan then slowly cook the sausages until golden brown all over. (You may need to work in batches.) Drain well on crumpled kitchen paper. Garnish with the deep-fried parsley sprigs and lemon wedges dusted with paprika.

Hard-boiled Eggs with Tuna Sauce

*The combination of eggs with a
tasty tuna mayonnaise makes a
nourishing first course that is quick
and easy to prepare.*

Serves 6

6 extra large eggs

200g/7oz can tuna in olive oil

3 anchovy fillets

15ml/1 tbsp capers, drained

lemon juice

30ml/2 tbsp olive oil

salt and ground black pepper

drained capers and anchovy fillets, to
   garnish (optional)

For the mayonnaise

1 egg yolk, at room temperature

5ml/1 tsp Dijon mustard

5ml/1 tsp white wine vinegar or
   lemon juice

150ml/¼ pint/⅔ cup olive oil

1   Boil the extra large eggs for
12–14 minutes. Drain under
cold running water. Peel carefully
and set aside.

2   Make the mayonnaise by
whisking the egg yolk, mustard
and white wine vinegar or lemon
juice together in a small bowl.
Whisk in the oil a few drops at a
time until 45–60ml/3–4 tbsp oil
have been incorporated. Pour in
the remaining oil in a slow stream,
whisking constantly.

3   Place the tuna with its oil, the
anchovies, capers, lemon juice
and olive oil in a blender or a food
processor. Process until smooth.

4   Fold the tuna mixture into the
mayonnaise. Season with black
pepper, and extra salt if necessary.
Chill for at least 1 hour.

5   To serve, cut the eggs in half
lengthwise. Arrange them on a
serving platter. Spoon over the
sauce, and garnish with capers and
anchovy fillets, if using. Serve the
eggs chilled.

Striped Fish Terrine

Serve this terrine cold or just warm, with a hollandaise sauce if you like.

INGREDIENTS

Serves 8

15ml/1 tbsp sunflower oil

450g/1lb salmon fillet, skinned

450g/1lb sole fillets, skinned

3 egg whites

105ml/7 tbsp double (heavy) cream

15ml/1 tbsp finely chopped fresh chives

juice of 1 lemon

115g/4oz/scant 1 cup fresh or frozen
    peas, cooked

5ml/1 tsp chopped fresh mint

salt, ground white pepper and
    grated nutmeg

thinly sliced cucumber, salad cress and
    whole chives, to garnish

1 Grease a 1 litre/1¾ pint/4 cup loaf tin (pan) or terrine with the oil. Slice the salmon thinly; cut it and the sole into long strips, 2.5cm/1in wide. Preheat the oven to 200°C/400°F/Gas 6.

2 Line the terrine neatly with alternate slices of salmon and sole leaving the ends overhanging the edge. You should be left with about one-third of the salmon and half the sole.

3 In a grease-free bowl, beat the egg whites with a pinch of salt until they form soft peaks. Purée the remaining sole in a food processor. Spoon into a mixing bowl, season, then fold in two-thirds of the egg whites, followed by two-thirds of the cream. Put half the mixture into a second bowl; stir in the chives. Add nutmeg to the first bowl.

4 Purée the remaining salmon, scrape it into a bowl; add the lemon juice. Fold in the remaining egg whites, followed by the remaining cream.

5 Purée the peas with the mint. Season the mixture and spread it over the base of the terrine, smoothing the surface with a spatula. Spoon over the sole with chives mixture and spread evenly.

6 Add the salmon mixture, then finish with the plain sole mixture. Cover with the overhanging fish fillets and make a lid of oiled foil. Stand the terrine in a roasting pan and pour in enough boiling water to come halfway up the sides.

7 Bake for 15–20 minutes, until the top fillets are just cooked and the mousse feels springy. Remove the foil, lay a wire rack over the top of the terrine and invert both rack and terrine on to a lipped baking sheet to catch the cooking juices that drain out. Keep these to make fish stock or soup.

8 Leaving the tin in place, let the terrine stand for about 15 minutes, then turn it over again, invert it on to a serving dish and lift off the tin carefully. Serve warm, or chill in the refrigerator first and serve cold. Garnish with thinly sliced cucumber, salad cress and chives before serving.

Golden Parmesan Chicken

Served warm or at room temperature, with the garlic-steeped mayonnaise, these tasty morsels make a great informal appetizer.

Serves 4

4 chicken breast fillets, skinned

75g/3oz/1½ cups fresh white
    breadcrumbs

40g/1½ oz Parmesan cheese, finely grated

30ml/2 tbsp chopped fresh parsley

2 eggs, beaten

120ml/4fl oz/½ cup good-quality
    mayonnaise

120ml/4fl oz/½ cup natural (plain) yogurt

1–2 garlic cloves, crushed

50g/2oz/4 tbsp butter, melted

salt and ground black pepper

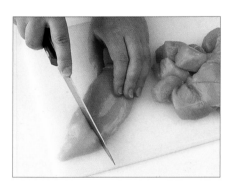

1 Cut each fillet into 4–5 chunks. Mix together the breadcrumbs, Parmesan, parsley and seasoning in a shallow dish.

2 Dip the chicken pieces in the egg, then into the breadcrumb mixture. Place in a single layer on a baking sheet; chill for 30 minutes.

3 Meanwhile, to make the garlic mayonnaise, mix together the mayonnaise, yogurt and garlic, and season to taste with ground black pepper. Spoon the mayonnaise into a small serving bowl. Chill until required.

4 Preheat the oven to 180°C/ 350°F/Gas 4. Drizzle the melted butter over the chicken pieces and cook them for about 20 minutes, until crisp and golden. Serve the chicken warm or at room temperature, accompanied by the garlic mayonnaise for dipping.

Chicken Croquettes

This recipe comes from Rebato's, a tapas bar in London. The chef there makes croquettes with a number of different flavourings; this version uses chicken.

Serves 4

25g/1oz/2 tbsp butter

25g/1oz/¼ cup plain (all-purpose) flour

150ml/¼ pint/⅔ cup milk

15ml/1 tbsp olive oil

1 boneless chicken breast portion with skin, about 75g/3oz, diced

1 garlic clove, finely chopped

1 small egg, beaten

50g/2oz/1 cup fresh white breadcrumbs

vegetable oil, for deep-frying

salt and ground black pepper

flat leaf parsley, to garnish

lemon wedges, to serve

1 Melt the butter in a small pan. Add the flour and cook gently, stirring, for 1 minute. Gradually beat in the milk to make a smooth, very thick sauce. Cover with a lid and remove the pan from the heat.

2 Heat the oil in a frying pan and cook the chicken with the garlic for 5 minutes, until the chicken is lightly browned and cooked through.

3 Turn the contents of the frying pan into a food processor or blender and process until finely chopped. Stir the chicken into the sauce, mixing it well. Add plenty of salt and pepper to taste. Leave to cool completely.

4 Shape into 8 even-size sausages, then dip each in egg and then breadcrumbs. Deep-fry in hot oil for 4 minutes until crisp and golden. Drain on kitchen paper and serve garnished with parsley and lemon wedges for squeezing.

Spicy Koftas

Cook these koftas in batches. After cooking keep each batch hot while you cook the rest.

INGREDIENTS

Makes 20–25

450g/1lb lean minced (ground) beef or lamb

30ml/2 tbsp finely ground ginger

30ml/2 tbsp finely ground garlic

4 green chillies, finely chopped

1 small onion, finely chopped

1 egg

2.5ml/½ tsp turmeric

5ml/1 tsp garam masala

50g/2oz chopped coriander (cilantro)

4–6 mint leaves, chopped

175g/6oz raw potato

salt, to taste

vegetable oil, for deep-frying

1 Place the beef or lamb in a large bowl along with the ginger, garlic, chillies, onion, egg, spices and herbs. Grate the potato into the bowl, and season with salt. Knead together to blend well and form a soft dough.

2 Using your fingers, shape the kofta mixture into portions the size of golf balls. You should be able to make 20–25 koftas. Leave the balls to rest at room temperature for about 25 minutes.

3 In a wok or frying pan, heat the oil to medium-hot and fry the koftas in small batches until they are golden brown in colour. Drain well and serve hot.

COOK'S TIP

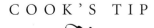

Leftover koftas can be coarsely chopped and packed into pitta bread spread with chutney or relish for a quick and delicious snack.

Pork Balls with a Minted Peanut Sauce

This recipe is equally delicious made with chicken breast portions.

Serves 4–6

275g/10oz leg of pork, trimmed and diced

1cm/½in piece fresh root ginger, grated

1 garlic clove, crushed

10ml/2 tsp sesame oil

15ml/1 tbsp medium-dry sherry

15ml/1 tbsp soy sauce

5ml/1 tsp sugar

1 egg white

2.5ml/½ tsp salt

pinch of white pepper

350g/12oz/scant 1¾ cups long grain rice, washed and cooked for 15 minutes

50g/2oz ham, diced

1 Iceberg or Gem (Bibb) lettuce, to serve

For the peanut sauce

15ml/1 tbsp creamed coconut (coconut cream)

75ml/2½fl oz/⅓ cup boiling water

30ml/2 tbsp smooth peanut butter

juice of 1 lime

1 red chilli, seeded and finely chopped

1 garlic clove, crushed

15ml/1 tbsp chopped fresh mint

15ml/1 tbsp chopped coriander (cilantro)

15ml/1 tbsp fish sauce (optional)

1 Place the pork, ginger and garlic in a food processor; process for 2–3 minutes until smooth. Add the sesame oil, sherry, soy sauce and sugar and blend with the pork mixture. Finally, add the egg white, salt and white pepper.

2 Spread the cooked rice and ham in a shallow dish. Using wet hands, shape the pork mixture into thumb-size balls. Roll in the rice to coat and pierce each ball with a bamboo skewer.

3 To make the sauce, put the creamed coconut in a measuring jug (cup) and cover with the boiling water. Place the peanut butter in another bowl with the lime juice, chilli, garlic, mint and coriander. Combine evenly then add the coconut and season with the fish sauce if using.

4 Place the pork balls in a bamboo steamer then steam over a pan of boiling water for 8–10 minutes. Arrange the pork balls on lettuce leaves on a plate with the sauce to one side.

Salads

Whether based on the freshest vegetables of the day, such as Spanish Salad with Olives and Capers, or a more filling grain and protein salad, like Egg and Fennel Tabbouleh with Nuts, salads are a vital part of every party meal, giving colour and texture, as well as taste.

Tomato and Feta Cheese Salad

Sweet, sun-ripened tomatoes are rarely more delicious than when served with feta cheese and olive oil.

INGREDIENTS

Serves 4

900g/2lb tomatoes
200g/7oz feta cheese
120ml/4fl oz/½ cup olive oil
12 black olives
4 fresh basil sprigs
ground black pepper

2 Slice the tomatoes thickly and arrange them attractively in a shallow serving dish.

3 Crumble the feta over the tomatoes, sprinkle with oil, then strew with the olives and basil sprigs. Season to taste with pepper and serve at room temperature.

1 Remove the tough cores from the tomatoes, using a small, sharp knife.

COOK'S TIP

Feta cheese has a strong flavour and can be salty. The least salty variety is imported from Greece and Turkey, and is available from specialist delicatessens.

Spinach and Roast Garlic Salad

Don't worry about the amount of garlic in this salad. During roasting, the garlic becomes sweet and subtle and loses its pungent taste.

INGREDIENTS

Serves 4

12 garlic cloves, unpeeled

60 ml/4 tbsp extra virgin olive oil

450g/1lb baby spinach leaves

50g/2oz/½ cup pine nuts, lightly toasted

juice of ½ lemon

salt and ground black pepper

1 Preheat the oven to 190°C/375°F/Gas 5. Place the garlic in a small roasting pan, toss in 30ml/2 tbsp of the olive oil and roast for about 15 minutes, until the garlic cloves are slightly charred around the edges.

2 While still warm, tip the garlic into a salad bowl. Add the spinach, pine nuts, lemon juice, remaining olive oil and a little salt. Toss well and add black pepper to taste. Serve immediately, inviting guests to squeeze the softened garlic purée out of the skin to eat.

Frisée Lettuce Salad with Bacon

This delicious salad may also be sprinkled with chopped hard-boiled egg.

INGREDIENTS

Serves 4

50g/2oz white bread

225g/8oz frisée lettuce or escarole leaves

75–90ml/5–6 tbsp extra virgin olive oil

175g/6oz piece smoked bacon, diced, or
    6 thick-cut smoked bacon rashers
    (strips), cut crossways into thin strips

1 small garlic clove, finely chopped

15ml/1 tbsp red wine vinegar

10ml/2 tsp Dijon mustard

salt and ground black pepper

1 Cut the bread into small cubes. Tear the frisée lettuce or escarole into bite-size pieces and put into a salad bowl.

2 Heat 15ml/1 tbsp of the oil in a medium, non-stick frying pan over a medium-low heat and add the bacon. Fry gently until well browned, stirring occasionally. Remove the bacon with a slotted spoon and drain on kitchen paper.

3 Add another 30ml/2 tbsp of the oil to the pan and fry the bread cubes over a medium-high heat, turning frequently, until evenly browned. Remove the bread cubes with a slotted spoon and drain on kitchen paper. Discard any remaining fat.

4 Stir the garlic, vinegar and mustard into the pan with the remaining oil and heat until just warm, whisking to combine. Season to taste, then pour the dressing over the salad and sprinkle with the fried bacon and croûtons. Serve immediately while still warm.

Coronation Salad

The famous salad dressing used in this dish was created especially for the coronation dinner of Queen Elizabeth II. It is a wonderful accompaniment to hard-boiled eggs and vegetables.

INGREDIENTS

Serves 6

450g/1lb new potatoes

45ml/3 tbsp French dressing

3 spring onions (scallions), chopped

6 eggs, hard-boiled (hard-cooked)
   and halved

frilly lettuce leaves

¼ cucumber, cut into thin strips

6 large radishes, sliced

1 carton salad cress

salt and ground black pepper

For the coronation dressing

30ml/2 tbsp olive oil

1 small onion, chopped

15ml/1 tbsp mild curry powder or korma
   spice mix

10ml/2 tsp tomato purée (paste)

30ml/2 tbsp lemon juice

30ml/2 tbsp sherry

300ml/½ pint/1¼ cups mayonnaise

150ml/¼ pint/⅔ cup plain yogurt

1 Boil the potatoes in salted water until tender. Drain them, transfer to a large bowl and toss in the French dressing while warm.

2 Stir in the spring onions and the salt and pepper, and allow to cool thoroughly.

3 Meanwhile, make the coronation dressing. Heat the oil in a small pan and fry the onion for 3 minutes, until soft. Stir in the curry powder or spice mix and fry for a further 1 minute. Remove from the heat and mix in all the other dressing ingredients.

4 Stir the dressing into the potatoes, add the eggs, then chill. Line a serving platter with lettuce leaves and pile the salad in the centre. Sprinkle over the cucumber, radishes and cress.

Turkish Salad

This classic salad is a wonderful combination of textures and flavours. The saltiness of the cheese is perfectly balanced by the refreshing salad vegetables.

INGREDIENTS

Serves 4

1 cos (romaine) lettuce heart
1 green (bell) pepper
1 red (bell) pepper
½ cucumber
4 tomatoes
1 red onion
225g/8oz/2 cups feta cheese, crumbled
black olives, to garnish

For the dressing
45ml/3 tbsp olive oil
45ml/3 tbsp lemon juice
1 garlic clove, crushed
15ml/1 tbsp chopped fresh parsley
15ml/1 tbsp chopped fresh mint
salt and ground black pepper

1 Chop the lettuce into bitesize pieces. Seed the peppers, remove the cores and cut the flesh into thin strips. Chop the cucumber and slice or chop the tomatoes. Cut the onion in half, then slice finely.

2 Place the chopped lettuce, peppers, cucumber, tomatoes and onion in a large bowl. Sprinkle the feta over the top and toss together lightly.

3 To make the dressing, blend together the olive oil, lemon juice and garlic in a small bowl. Stir in the chopped parsley and mint and season with salt and pepper to taste.

4 Pour the dressing over the salad and toss lightly. Garnish with a handful of black olives and serve immediately.

Persian Salad

This very simple salad can be served with almost any dish. Don't add the dressing until just before you are ready to serve.

INGREDIENTS

Serves 4

4 tomatoes
½ cucumber
1 onion
1 cos (romaine) lettuce heart

For the dressing
30ml/2 tbsp olive oil
juice of 1 lemon
1 garlic clove, crushed
salt and ground black pepper

1 Cut the tomatoes and cucumber into small cubes. Finely chop the onion and tear the lettuce into pieces.

2 Place the prepared tomatoes, cucumber, onion and lettuce in a large salad bowl and mix lightly together.

3 To make the dressing, pour the olive oil into a small bowl. Add the lemon juice, garlic and seasoning and blend together well.

4 Pour over the salad and toss lightly to mix. Sprinkle with extra black pepper and serve.

Fennel Coleslaw

The fennel, with its aniseed flavour, makes this refreshing salad quite different from standard coleslaw.

INGREDIENTS

Serves 4

175g/6oz fennel

2 spring onions (scallions)

175g/6oz white cabbage

115g/4oz celery

175g/6oz carrots

50g/2oz/scant ½ cup sultanas (golden raisins)

15ml/1 tbsp chopped fresh parsley

45ml/3 tbsp extra virgin olive oil

5ml/1 tsp lemon juice

shreds of spring onion, to garnish

3 Stir in the chopped parsley, olive oil and lemon juice. Mix all the ingredients very thoroughly. Cover and chill in the refrigerator for 3 hours to allow the flavours to mingle. Serve garnished with shreds of spring onion.

1 Using a sharp knife, cut the fennel and spring onions into thin slices.

2 Slice the cabbage and celery finely and cut the carrots into fine strips. Place in a serving bowl together with the fennel and spring onions. Add the sultanas and toss lightly to mix.

Green Bean and Sweet Red Pepper Salad

Serrano chillies are very fiery so be cautious about their use.

Serves 4

350g/12oz cooked green beans, quartered

2 red (bell) peppers, seeded and chopped

2 spring onions (scallions), chopped

1 or more drained pickled serrano chillies, rinsed, seeded and chopped

1 Iceberg lettuce, coarsely shredded

olives, to garnish

For the dressing

45ml/3 tbsp red wine vinegar

135ml/9 tbsp olive oil

salt and ground black pepper

1 Combine the cooked green beans, chopped peppers, chopped spring onions and chillies in a salad bowl.

2 Make the salad dressing. Pour the red wine vinegar into a bowl or jug. Add salt and ground black pepper to taste, then gradually whisk in the olive oil until well combined.

3 Pour the salad dressing over the prepared vegetables and toss lightly together to mix and coat thoroughly.

4 Line a large serving platter with the shredded Iceberg lettuce leaves and arrange the salad vegetables attractively on top. Garnish with the olives and serve.

Orange and Red Onion Salad with Cumin

Cumin and mint give this refreshing first course a Middle Eastern flavour.

Serves 6

6 oranges

2 red onions

15ml/1 tbsp cumin seeds

5ml/1 tsp coarsely ground black pepper

15ml/1 tbsp chopped fresh mint

90ml/6 tbsp olive oil

salt

To serve

fresh mint sprigs

black olives

1 Slice the oranges thinly, working over a bowl to catch any juice. Then, holding each orange slice in turn over the bowl, cut round with scissors to remove the peel and pith. Slice the onions thinly and separate the rings.

2 Arrange the orange and onion slices in layers in a shallow dish, sprinkling each layer with cumin seeds, black pepper, mint, olive oil and salt to taste. Pour over the orange juice collected when slicing the oranges.

3 Leave the salad to marinate in a cool place for about 2 hours. Just before serving, sprinkle the salad with the mint sprigs and black olives.

Spanish Salad with Olives and Capers

Make this refreshing salad in the summer when tomatoes are sweet and full of flavour. The dressing gives it a lovely tang.

Serves 4

4 tomatoes

1/2 cucumber

1 bunch spring onions (scallions)

1 bunch watercress

8 pimiento-stuffed olives

30ml/2 tbsp drained capers

For the dressing

30ml/2 tbsp red wine vinegar

5ml/1 tsp paprika

2.5ml/1/2 tsp ground cumin

1 garlic clove, crushed

75ml/5 tbsp olive oil

salt and ground black pepper

1 To peel the tomatoes, place them in a heatproof bowl, add boiling water to cover and leave for 1 minute. Lift out with a slotted spoon and plunge into a bowl of cold water. Leave for 1 minute, then drain. Slip the skins off the tomatoes and dice the flesh finely. Put in a salad bowl.

2 Peel the cucumber, dice it finely and add it to the tomatoes. Trim and chop half the spring onions, add them to the salad bowl and mix lightly.

3 Break the watercress into small sprigs. Add to the tomato mixture, with the olives and capers.

4 Make the dressing. Mix the wine vinegar, paprika, cumin and garlic in a bowl. Whisk in the oil and add salt and pepper to taste. Pour over the salad and toss lightly to coat. Serve with the remaining spring onions on the side.

Egg and Fennel Tabbouleh with Nuts

Tabbouleh is a Middle Eastern salad of steamed bulgur wheat, flavoured with lots of parsley, mint and garlic.

Serves 4

250g/9oz/1¼ cups bulgur wheat
4 small (US medium) eggs
1 fennel bulb
1 bunch spring onions
   (scallions), chopped
25g/1oz/½ cup sun-dried tomatoes, sliced
45ml/3 tbsp chopped fresh parsley
30ml/2 tbsp chopped fresh mint
75g/3oz/½ cup black olives
60ml/4 tbsp olive oil, preferably Greek
   or Spanish
30ml/2 tbsp garlic oil
30ml/2 tbsp lemon juice
salt and ground black pepper

1 Cover the bulgur wheat with boiling water and leave to soak for 15 minutes. Transfer to a metal sieve, place over a pan of boiling water, cover and steam for 10 minutes. Spread out on a metal tray and leave to cool while you cook the eggs and fennel.

2 Hard-boil (hard-cook) the small eggs for 8 minutes. Cool under running water, peel and quarter, or, using an egg slicer, slice not quite all the way through.

3 Halve and then finely slice the fennel. Boil in salted water for 6 minutes, drain and cool under running water.

4 Combine the egg quarters, fennel, spring onions, sun-dried tomatoes, parsley, mint and olives with the bulgur wheat. If you have sliced the eggs, arrange them on top of the salad. Dress the tabbouleh with olive oil, garlic oil and lemon juice. Season well.

COOK'S TIP
Small whole eggs, such as gull's, quail's, plover's or guinea fowl's, would be good in this dish.

Cracked Wheat Salad

Fresh herbs, bursting with the flavours of summer, are essential for this salad. Dried herbs are not a suitable substitute.

INGREDIENTS

Serves 4

225g/8oz/1⅓ cups cracked wheat

350ml/12fl oz/1½ cups vegetable stock

1 cinnamon stick

generous pinch of ground cumin

pinch of cayenne pepper

pinch of ground cloves

5ml/1 tsp salt

10 mangetouts (snow peas), trimmed

1 red and 1 yellow (bell) pepper, roasted, skinned, seeded and diced

2 plum tomatoes, peeled, seeded and diced

2 shallots, finely sliced

5 black olives, pitted and cut into quarters

30ml/2 tbsp each shredded fresh basil, mint and parsley

30ml/2 tbsp roughly chopped walnuts

30ml/2 tbsp balsamic vinegar

120ml/4f loz/½ cup extra virgin olive oil

ground black pepper

onion rings, to garnish

1 Place the cracked wheat in a large bowl. Pour the stock into a pan and bring to the boil with the spices and salt.

2 Cook for 1 minute, then pour the stock, with the cinnamon stick, over the cracked wheat. Leave to stand for 30 minutes.

3 In another bowl, mix together the mangetouts, peppers, tomatoes, shallots, olives, herbs and walnuts. Add the vinegar, olive oil and a little black pepper and stir thoroughly to mix.

4 Strain the cracked wheat of any liquid and discard the cinnamon stick. Place the cracked wheat in a serving bowl, stir in the fresh vegetable mixture and serve, garnished with onion rings.

Potato Salad with Curry Plant Mayonnaise

Potato salad can be made well in advance and is therefore a useful dish for serving as an unusual appetizer at a party. Its popularity means that there are very rarely any leftovers to be cleared away at the end of the day.

INGREDIENTS

Serves 6

1kg/2¼lb new potatoes, in skins

300ml/½ pint/1¼ cups store-bought mayonnaise

6 curry plant leaves, roughly chopped

salt and ground black pepper

mixed lettuce leaves or other salad greens, to serve

1 Place the potatoes in a pan of salted water, bring to the boil and cook for 15 minutes or until tender. Drain and place in a large bowl to cool slightly.

2 Mix the mayonnaise with the curry plant leaves and black pepper. Stir these into the potatoes while they are still warm. Leave to cool completely, then serve on a bed of mixed lettuce leaves or other assorted salad leaves.

Smoked Trout Pasta Salad

The little pasta shells catch the trout,
creating tasty mouthfuls.

Serves 8

15g/½oz/1 tbsp butter
175g/6oz/1 cup minced (ground)
  bulb fennel
6 spring onions (scallions), 2 minced
  (ground) and the rest thinly sliced
225g/8oz skinless smoked trout
  fillets, flaked
45ml/3 tbsp chopped fresh dill
120ml/4fl oz/½ cup mayonnaise
10ml/2 tsp fresh lemon juice
30ml/2 tbsp whipping cream
450g/1lb/4 cups small pasta shapes
salt and ground black pepper
dill sprigs, to garnish

1 Melt the butter in a small pan. Cook the fennel and minced onions for 3–5 minutes. Transfer to a bowl to cool slightly.

2 Add the sliced spring onions, trout, dill, mayonnaise, lemon juice and cream. Season and mix.

3 Bring a large pan of water to the boil. Salt to taste and add the pasta. Cook according to the instructions on the packet until just *al dente*. Drain thoroughly and leave to cool.

4 Add the pasta to the vegetable and trout mixture and toss to coat evenly. Taste for seasoning. Serve the salad lightly chilled or at room temperature, garnished with sprigs of dill.

Pasta, Olive and Avocado Salad

The ingredients of this salad are united by a wonderful sun-dried tomato and fresh basil dressing.

INGREDIENTS

Serves 6

225g/8oz pasta spirals or other small
 pasta shapes
115g/4oz can sweetcorn, drained, or
 frozen sweetcorn, thawed
1/2 red (bell) pepper, seeded and diced
8 black olives, pitted and sliced
3 spring onions (scallions), finely chopped
2 medium avocados

For the dressing

2 sun-dried tomato halves, loose-packed
 (not preserved in oil)
25ml/1½ tbsp balsamic or white
 wine vinegar
25ml/1½ tbsp red wine vinegar
1/2 garlic clove, crushed
2.5ml/1/2 tsp salt
75ml/5 tbsp olive oil
15ml/1 tbsp chopped fresh basil

1 To make the dressing, drop the sun-dried tomatoes into a pan containing 2.5cm/1in boiling water and simmer for about 3 minutes until tender. Drain and chop finely.

2 Combine the sun-dried tomatoes, both vinegars, garlic and salt in a food processor. With the machine on, add the olive oil in a stream. Stir in the basil.

3 Cook the pasta in a large pan of boiling salted water until *al dente*. Drain well. In a large bowl, combine the pasta, sweetcorn, red pepper, olives and spring onions. Add the dressing and toss well.

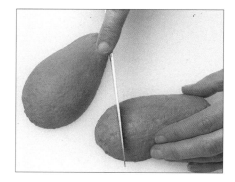

4 Just before serving, peel and stone (pit) the avocados, then cut the flesh into cubes. Mix gently into the pasta then place the salad on a serving dish. Serve at room temperature.

Devilled Ham and Pineapple Salad

This tasty salad, with a crunchy topping of toasted almonds, is quick to prepare.

INGREDIENTS

Serves 4

225g/8oz whole-wheat penne

150ml/¼ pint/⅔ cup natural
   (plain) yogurt

15ml/1 tbsp cider vinegar

5ml/1 tsp wholegrain mustard

large pinch of caster (superfine) sugar

30ml/2 tbsp hot mango chutney

115g/4oz cooked lean ham, cubed

200g/7oz can pineapple chunks, drained

2 celery sticks, chopped

½ green (bell) pepper, seeded and diced

15ml/1 tbsp toasted flaked (sliced)
   almonds, chopped roughly

salt and ground black pepper

crusty bread, to serve

1 Cook the pasta in a large pan of salted boiling water until *al dente*. Drain and rinse thoroughly. Leave to cool.

2 To make the dressing, mix the yogurt, vinegar, mustard, sugar and mango chutney together. Season with salt and pepper. Add the pasta and toss lightly together.

3 Transfer the pasta to a serving dish. Add the ham, pineapple, celery and green pepper.

4 Sprinkle toasted almonds over the top of the salad. Serve with crusty bread.

Desserts

Depending on the rest of the party meal, desserts can range from the simple but elegant Watermelon, Ginger and Grapefruit Salad to the elaborate Iced Praline Torte. Fruit tarts refreshingly top off a heavier meal, but few guests will be able to resist the temptation of a Chocolate Mandarin Trifle.

Cool Green Fruit Salad

A sophisticated, simple fruit salad for any time of the year.

INGREDIENTS

Serves 6

3 Ogen or Honeydew melons

115g/4oz seedless green grapes

2 kiwi fruit

1 star fruit

1 green-skinned eating apple

1 lime

175ml/6fl oz/¾ cup sparkling grape juice

1 Cut the melons in half and remove the seeds. Keeping the shells intact, scoop out the flesh with a melon baller, or scoop it out using a spoon and cut into bite size cubes. Reserve the melon shells.

2 Remove any stems from the grapes and, if they are large, cut them in half. Peel and chop the kiwi fruit. Thinly slice the star fruit. Core and thinly slice the apple and place in a mixing bowl with the melon, grapes, kiwi fruit and star fruit.

3 Thinly pare the rind from the lime and cut it in fine strips. Blanch the lime strips in boiling water for 30 seconds, drain and rinse in cold water. Squeeze the juice from the lime and toss it into the bowl of fruit.

4 Spoon the prepared fruit into the reserved melon shells and chill the shells in the refrigerator until required. Just before serving, spoon the sparkling grape juice over the fruit and sprinkle with the strips of lime rind.

COOK'S TIP

On a hot summer's day, serve the filled melon shells nestling on a platter of crushed ice to keep them beautifully cool.

Watermelon, Ginger and Grapefruit Salad

This pretty, pink combination is very light and refreshing for any summer meal.

INGREDIENTS

Serves 4

450g/1lb/2 cups watermelon flesh
2 ruby or pink grapefruit
2 pieces stem (crystallized) ginger and
   30ml/2 tbsp of the syrup

1 Remove any seeds from the watermelon and cut the flesh into bitesize chunks.

2 Using a small, sharp knife, cut away all the peel and white pith from the grapefruit and carefully lift out the segments, catching any juice in a bowl.

COOK'S TIP

Toss the fruits gently – grapefruit segments will break up easily and the appearance of the dish will be spoiled.

3 Finely chop the stem ginger and place it in a serving bowl with the melon cubes and grapefruit segments, adding the reserved juice.

4 Spoon over the ginger syrup and toss the fruits lightly to mix. Chill before serving.

Clementines in Cinnamon Caramel

The combination of sweet, yet sharp clementines and caramel sauce is divine. Served with yogurt or crème fraîche, this makes a delicious dessert.

INGREDIENTS

Serves 4–6

8–12 clementines
225g/8oz/generous 1 cup granulated sugar
2 cinnamon sticks
30ml/2 tbsp orange-flavoured liqueur
25g/1oz/¼ cup shelled pistachio nuts

1 Pare the rind from 2 clementines using a vegetable peeler and cut it into fine strips. Set aside.

2 Peel the clementines, removing all the pith from them but keeping them intact. Put the fruits in a serving bowl.

3 Gently heat the sugar in a pan until it melts and turns a rich golden brown. Immediately turn off the heat.

4 Cover your hand with a dishtowel and pour in 300ml/ ½ pint/1¼ cups warm water (the mixture will bubble and splutter). Bring slowly to the boil, stirring until the caramel has dissolved. Add the shredded peel and cinnamon sticks, then simmer for 5 minutes. Stir in the orange-flavoured liqueur.

5 Leave the syrup to cool for about 10 minutes, then pour over the clementines. Cover the bowl and chill for several hours or overnight.

6 Blanch the pistachio nuts in boiling water. Drain, cool and remove the dark outer skins. Sprinkle over the clementines and serve immediately.

Death by Chocolate

One of the richest chocolate cakes ever, so serve in thin slices.

INGREDIENTS

Serves 16–20

225g/8oz plain dark (bittersweet)
   chocolate, broken into squares
115g/4oz/½ cup unsalted butter
150ml/¼ pint/⅔ cup milk
225g/8oz/1¼ cups light muscovado
   (molasses) sugar
10ml/2 tsp vanilla essence (extract)
2 eggs, separated
150ml/¼ pint/⅔ cup sour cream
225g/8oz/2 cups self-raising flour
5ml/1tsp baking powder (soda)

For the filling
60ml/4 tbsp seedless rasperry jam
60ml/4 tbsp brandy
400g/14oz plain dark (bittersweet)
   chocolate, broken into squares
200g/7oz/scant 1 cup unsalted butter

For the topping
250ml/8fl oz/1 cup double (heavy) cream
225g/8oz plain dark (bittersweet)
   chocolate, broken into squares
chocolate curls, to decorate
chocolate-dipped physalis (Cape
   gooseberries) to serve (optional)

1 Preheat the oven to 180°C/350F/ Gas 4. Grease and base-line a deep 23cm/9in springform cake tin. Place the chocolate, butter and milk in a saucepan and heat until smooth. Remove from the heat and beat in sugar and vanilla.

2 Beat the egg yolks and cream in a bowl, then beat into the chocolate mixture. Sift the flour and baking powder over the surface and fold in. Whisk the egg whites in a grease-free bowl until stiff; fold into the mixture.

3 Scrape into the prepared tin and bake for 45-55 minutes, or until firm to the touch. Cool in the tin for 15 minutes, then invert to a wire rack to cool.

4 Slice the cold cake horizon- tally to make three even layers. In a small pan, warm the jam with 15ml/1 tbsp of the brandy, then brush over two of the layers. Heat the remaining brandy in a pan with the chocolate and butter, stirring, until smooth. Cool until beginning to thicken.

5 Spread the bottom layer of the cake with half the chocolate filling, taking care not to disturb the jam. Top with a second layer, jam side up, and spread with the remaining filling. Top with the final layer and press lightly. Leave to set.

6 To make the topping, heat the cream and chocolate together in a pan over a low heat, stirring frequently until the chocolate has melted. Pour into a bowl, leave to cool, then whisk until the mixture begins to hold its shape.

7 Spread the top and sides of the cake with the chocolate ganache. Decorate with chocolate curls and, if liked, chocolate-dipped physalis (Cape gooseberries).

Raspberry Meringue Gâteau

A hazelnut meringue sandwiched with whipped cream and raspberries makes an irresistible dessert.

INGREDIENTS

Serves 6

4 egg whites

225g/8oz/1 cup caster (superfine) sugar

a few drops of vanilla essence (extract)

5ml/1 tsp distilled malt vinegar

115g/4oz/1 cup roasted and chopped
    hazelnuts, ground

300ml/½ pint/1¼ cups double
    (heavy) cream

350g/12oz/2 cups raspberries

icing (confectioners') sugar, for dusting

raspberries and mint sprigs, to decorate

For the sauce

225g/8oz/1⅓ cups raspberries

45–60ml/3–4 tbsp icing (confectioner's)
    sugar, sifted

15ml/1 tbsp orange liqueur

1 Preheat the oven to 180°C/
350°F/Gas 4. Grease 2
20cm/8in sandwich tins (pans)
and line the bases with
greaseproof (waxed) paper.

2 Whisk the egg whites in a large
bowl until they hold stiff peaks,
then gradually whisk in the caster
sugar a tablespoon at a time,
whisking well after each addition.

COOK'S TIP

~

You can buy roasted chopped
hazelnuts in supermarkets.
Otherwise toast whole hazelnuts
under the grill (broiler) and rub
off the flaky skins using a clean
dishtowel. To chop finely, process
in a blender or food processor for a
few moments.

3 Continue whisking the
meringue mixture for a minute
or two until very stiff, then fold in
the vanilla essence, vinegar and
ground hazelnuts.

4 Divide the meringue mixture
between the prepared
sandwich tins and spread level.
Bake for 50–60 minutes, until crisp.
Remove the meringues from the
tins and leave them to cool on a
wire rack.

5 While the meringues are
cooling, make the sauce.
Process the raspberries with the
icing sugar and orange liqueur in a
blender or food processor, then
press the purée through a fine
nylon sieve to remove any pips
(seeds). Chill the sauce until ready
to serve.

6 Whip the cream until it forms
soft peaks, then gently fold in
the raspberries. Sandwich the
meringue rounds together with the
raspberry cream.

7 Dust the top of the gâteau with
icing sugar. Decorate with
mint sprigs and serve with the
raspberry sauce.

VARIATION

Fresh redcurrants make a good
alternative to raspberries. Pick over
the fruit, then pull each sprig
gently through the prongs of a fork
to release the redcurrants. Add
them to the whipped cream with a
little icing sugar, to taste.

Raspberry Tart

This glazed fruit tart really does taste as good as it looks.

Serves 8

4 egg yolks
65g/2½ oz/⅓ cup granulated sugar
45ml/3 tbsp plain (all-purpose) flour
300ml/½ pint/1¼ cups milk
pinch of salt
2.5ml/½ tsp vanilla essence (extract)
450g/1lb fresh raspberries
75ml/5 tbsp grape or redcurrant jelly
15ml/1 tbsp fresh orange juice

For the pastry

150g/5oz/1¼ cups plain
    (all-purpose) flour
2.5ml/½ tsp baking powder (soda)
1.5ml/¼ tsp salt
15ml/1 tbsp caster (superfine) sugar
grated rind of ½ orange
90ml/6 tbsp cold butter, cut in pieces
1 egg yolk
45–60ml/3–4 tbsp whipping cream

1 For the pastry, sift the dry ingredients into a bowl. Stir in the orange rind then add the butter and mix until the mixture resembles coarse crumbs. Stir in the egg yolk and just enough cream to bind the dough. Gather into a ball, wrap in greaseproof (waxed) paper and chill.

2 For the custard filling, beat the egg yolks and sugar until thick and lemon-coloured. Gradually stir in the flour. In a pan, bring the milk and salt just to the boil, and remove from the heat. Whisk into the egg yolk mixture, return to the pan, and continue whisking over medium high heat until just bubbling. Cook for 3 minutes to thicken. Transfer immediately to a bowl. Stir in the vanilla to blend.

3 Cover with greaseproof paper to prevent a skin from forming.

4 Preheat the oven to 200°C/ 400°F/Gas 6. On a lightly floured surface, roll out the dough about 3mm/⅛in thick, transfer to a 25cm/10in flan tin and trim the edge. Prick the bottom all over with a fork and line with greaseproof paper. Fill with baking beans and bake for 15 minutes. Remove the paper and baking beans. Continue baking until golden, 6–8 minutes more. Let cool.

5 Spread an even layer of the custard filling in the tart shell and arrange the raspberries on top. Melt the jelly and orange juice in a pan over a low heat and brush on top to glaze.

Kiwi Ricotta Cheese Tart

*It is worth taking your time
arranging the topping in neat rows
for this impressive-looking tart.*

INGREDIENTS

Serves 8

50g/2oz/½ cup blanched almonds

90g/3½oz/½ cup plus 15ml/1 tbsp
    caster (superfine) sugar

900g/2lb/4 cups ricotta cheese

250ml/8fl oz/1 cup whipping cream

1 egg

3 egg yolks

15ml/1 tbsp plain (all-purpose) flour

pinch of salt

30ml/2 tbsp rum

grated rind of 1 lemon

40ml/2½ tbsp lemon juice

50ml/2fl oz/¼ cup clear honey

5 kiwi fruit

For the pastry

150g/5oz/1¼ cups plain
    (all-purpose) flour

15ml/1 tbsp granulated sugar

2.5ml/½ tsp salt

2.5ml/½ tsp baking powder

75g/3oz/6 tbsp cold butter, cut in pieces

1 egg yolk

45–60ml/3–4 tbsp whipping cream

1 For the pastry, sift the flour, sugar, salt and baking powder into a bowl. Cut in the butter until the mixture resembles coarse crumbs. Mix the egg yolk and cream. Stir in just enough to bind the dough.

2 Transfer to a lightly floured surface, flatten slightly, wrap in greaseproof (waxed) paper and chill for 30 minutes. Preheat the oven to 220°C/425°F/Gas 7.

3 On a floured surface, roll out the dough 3mm/⅛in thick and transfer to a 23cm/9in springform tin (pan). Crimp the edge.

4 Prick the bottom of the dough all over with a fork. Line with greaseproof paper and fill with baking beans. Bake for 10 minutes. Remove the paper and beans and bake until golden, 6–8 minutes more. Let cool. Reduce the heat to 180°C/350°F/Gas 4.

5 Grind the almonds finely with 15ml/1 tbsp of the sugar in a food processor or blender.

6 With an electric mixer, beat the ricotta until creamy. Add the cream, egg, yolks, remaining sugar, flour, salt, rum, lemon rind and 30ml/2 tbsp of the lemon juice. Beat to combine.

7 Stir in the ground almonds until well blended.

8 Pour into the shell and bake until golden, about 1 hour. Let cool, then chill, loosely covered, for 2–3 hours. Unmould and place on a serving plate.

9 Combine the honey and remaining lemon juice for the glaze. Set aside.

10 Peel the kiwis. Halve them lengthwise, then cut crosswise into 5mm/¼in slices. Arrange the slices in rows across the top of the tart. Just before serving, brush with the glaze.

Chocolate Mandarin Trifle

Trifle is always a tempting treat, but when a rich chocolate and mascarpone custard is combined with Amaretto and mandarin oranges, it becomes irresistible.

INGREDIENTS

Serves 6–8

4 trifle sponges (ladyfingers or pound
    cake slices)
14 amaretti or almond biscuits (cookies)
60ml/4 tbsp Amaretto di Sarone
    or sweet sherry
8 mandarin oranges

For the custard

200g/7oz plain (semisweet) chocolate,
    broken into squares
30ml/2 tbsp cornflour (cornstarch) or
    custard powder
30ml/2 tbsp caster (superfine) sugar
2 egg yolks
200ml/7fl oz/1 cup milk
250g/9oz/generous 1 cup mascarpone

For the topping

280ml/10fl oz/250g/9oz/generous 1 cup
    whipped cream
chocolate shapes
mandarin slices

1 Break up the trifle sponges and place them in a large glass serving dish. Crumble the amaretti over and then sprinkle with Amaretto or sweet sherry.

2 Squeeze the juice from 2 of the mandarins and sprinkle into the dish. Segment the rest and put in the dish.

3 Make the custard. Melt the chocolate in a heatproof bowl over hot water. In a separate bowl, mix the cornflour or custard powder, sugar and egg yolks to a smooth paste.

4 Heat the milk in a small pan until it is almost boiling, then pour in a steady stream on to the egg yolk mixture, stirring constantly. Return to the clean pan and stir over a low heat until the custard has thickened slightly and is smooth.

5 Stir in the mascarpone until melted, then add the melted chocolate, mixing it thoroughly. Spread evenly over the trifle, cool, then chill until set.

6 To finish, spread the whipped cream over the custard, then decorate with chocolate shapes and the remaining mandarin slices just before serving.

COOK'S TIP

Always use the best chocolate, which has a high percentage of cocoa solids, and take care not to overheat the chocolate when melting as it will lose its gloss and look "grainy".

Iced Praline Torte

This elaborate torte can be made days ahead and frozen. Allow the torte to stand at room temperature for an hour before serving.

INGREDIENTS

Serves 8

115g/4oz/1 cup almonds or hazelnuts

115g/4oz/8 tbsp caster (superfine) sugar

115g/4oz/⅔ cup raisins

90ml/6 tbsp rum or brandy

115g/4oz dark (bittersweet) chocolate,

30ml/2 tbsp milk

450ml/¾ pint/scant 2 cups double (heavy) cream

30ml/2 tbsp strong black coffee

16 sponge-finger biscuits (lady fingers or pound cake slices)

To finish

150ml/¼ pint/⅔ cup double (heavy) cream

50g/2oz/½ cup flaked (sliced) almonds, toasted

15g/½oz dark (bittersweet) chocolate, melted

1 To make the praline, have ready an oiled cake tin (pan) or baking sheet. Put the nuts into a heavy pan with the sugar and heat gently until the sugar melts. Swirl the pan to coat the nuts in the hot sugar. Cook slowly until the nuts brown and the sugar caramelizes. Transfer the nuts quickly to the tin or tray and leave them to cool completely. Break them up and grind them to a fine powder in a blender or food processor.

2 Soak the raisins in 45ml/3 tbsp of the rum or brandy for at least an hour, so they soften and absorb the rum. Break up the chocolate and melt with the milk in a bowl over a pan of hot, but not boiling water. Remove and allow to cool. Lightly grease a 1.2 litre/ 2 pint/5 cup loaf tin (pan) and line it with greaseproof (waxed) paper.

3 Whisk the cream in a bowl until it holds soft peaks. Whisk in the cold chocolate. Then fold in the praline and the soaked raisins, with any liquid.

4 Mix the coffee and remaining rum or brandy in a shallow dish. Dip in the sponge fingers and arrange half in a layer over the base of the prepared loaf tin.

5 Cover with the chocolate mixture and add another layer of soaked sponge fingers. Leave in the freezer overnight.

6 Whip the double cream for the topping. Dip the tin briefly into warm water to loosen it and turn the torte out on to a serving plate. Cover with the whipped cream, sprinkle the top with toasted flaked almonds and drizzle the melted chocolate over the top. Return the torte to the freezer until it is needed.

COOK'S TIP

Make the praline in advance and store it in an airtight jar until needed.

Index